Roaming, Rambling, and Reminiscing

Musings from a South Georgia Mule Wagon

J. D. PORTER

Roaming, Rambling, and Reminiscing: Musings from a South Georgia Mule Wagon by J. D. Porter

Copyright © 2024 by J.D. Porter

All rights reserved. No part of this book may be reproduced or used in any manner without written permission of the copyright owner except for the use of quotations in a book review.

First paperback edition 2024
Book design by Jessica Reed

ISBN 978-1-7353155-4-6 (paperback)
ISBN 978-1-7353155-5-3 (ebook)

www.jdporterbooks.com

To the readers of the *Albany Herald* and
to newspaper subscribers everywhere.

Because local news is essential to a healthy democracy.

ALSO BY J. D. PORTER

Fiction:

The Menagerie, A Zoo Story

The Dogcatcher and the Fox

Non-fiction:

*The View from a Wagon:
Five Lessons for Living Life in the Slow Lane*

*Lessons from the Zoo:
Ten Animals That Changed My Life*

Table of Contents

Forward	7
Introduction	11
Giddy Up, Mule	13
A Peaceful Pace	15
Working on Mule Time	17
The View from a Wagon: As Natural as Life	20
Off the Beaten Path	23
Shotguns: Tools of the Trade	25
Southerners Tend to Slow Life Down	28
Standing Up for What's Right	31
An Ode to Joy	33
The Dog's Nose Knows	36
Diggory the Greyhound: Canine Royalty	39
Therapy Dogs	44
The Dogs of War	47
Guard Dogs Protect the Property We Claim	50
Herding Dogs Are Intelligent, Hard-Working Canines	53
A Time to Stop and Smell the Flowers	57
Creating New Rituals in the Time of the Coronavirus Pandemic	60
Wrens in the Driveway	64
Celebrating Earth Day at Fifty	67
On the Verge of a Coronavirus Book Crisis	70
Feeling Squirrely?	73
The Art of the Walk	77
Urban Deer: Walking the Fine Line between Natural Beauty and Pest	79
Box Turtles 'Fred', 'Wilma' Represent the Quiet Life	82

Contents, continued

Lizards in our Midst	85
The 'Joy' of Thanksgiving	88
A Sign of the Times	91
Dogs on the Hunt	94
The Search for a Fitting Final Legacy	100
At Home with the Gnomes	103
Let the Walking Man Walk	106
The Right to Roam…Good for the Soul	109
The Matriarch—A Mother's Day Tribute	112
The Silverback—A Father's Day Tribute	115
These 'Flying Primates' Have Something to Crow About	119
Why Did It Have to Be Snakes?	122
'Shroomage…from Portobellos to Death Angels to Dog Vomit	125
If I Could Talk to the Animals…	128
Beginning the Slow Process of Saying Farewell	131
The Southern Plantation	134
The Fire Bird	138
The Tortoise and the Billionaire	141
Ready to Live a Life in the Fast Lane	145
Horace King, the Bridge Builder	148
Being Part of the "Village"	154
Contemplating Tombstones and Our Burial Rituals	157
Letters from the Heart	161
Cemeteries: Stories Etched in Stone	164

Forward

In Everytown, USA—every small hamlet, burg, community...every place that at least a few people call home, there are essential figures who give those places their character, who, through skills possessed by few of their townsmen or through unique artistic gifts, help define the essence of such places. These individuals rarely leave behind evidence of their passage outside the places that claim them, but they become crucial elements of those places.

Doug Porter long will be remembered as such a vital part of Albany in southwest Georgia. Sure, Doug's impact as director of the zoo at Albany-based Chehaw Park & Zoo—a facility dreamed to life by former Mutual of Omaha's Wild Kingdom stalwart Jim Fowler...you remember him, the guy who wrestled with the 20-foot boa constrictor while Marlin Perkins watched from a safe distance away?—one of many such facilities on which he built his career, was significant in the community that he adopted as home and in turn adopted him as its own. But it was what Doug did after he hung up his Chehaw hat that richly endeared him to a metropolitan area that has the feel and overarching mentality of a small town.

A man possessing an unlimited supply of energy and whose travels and studies had afforded him a keen intellect and a touch of the wanderlust that kept him from settling into that post-retirement malaise that impacts so many of his contemporaries, Doug staked out an even wider local acclaim by writing about a way of life that had, through that funny way that fate has of doing things, morphed from necessity into a plaything of the well-to-do.

Those necessary treks into the wooded acres where native wild game matched wits with sometimes desperate hunters whose daily meals depended on their weaponry skills in the south Georgia woods were, by the time Doug retired, part of a world-renowned modern-day plantation system whereby the captains of industry traipsed in search of the bounty of the land—and, it should be noted, their presumed manhood—in an industry that has a yearly economic impact on the region measured in the hundreds of millions of dollars. A learned man who studied the ways of those long-ago hunters and trappers, Doug joined the new-world aristocracy in those South Georgia woods, not in the search for trophies and bragging rights but as the driver of a throwback mule wagon, once an essential part of the plantation life.

It wasn't enough for this lover of nature and its creatures to tag along and perhaps live vicariously through the exploits of the modern "outdoorsmen." His was to play a part that allowed him to take in the essence of the hunt…from those who were there in search of a trophy to the plantation staff that cared for the animals and habitat of the game to the tradition-rich duties of the mule wagon driver who lent the process a heaping helping of history while proving invaluable in caring for the details that can make or break such an excursion.

That Doug decided to share the stories of the hunt—from the seat of the mule-drawn wagon, as it was—revealed his gifts for storytelling and the written word and endeared him to a population hungry for such tales. Doug became their eyes and ears of the hunt, relating the sometimes hilarious, sometimes touching and always revealing stories that helped keep alive a part of the region that was being relegated to an all-but-forgotten past and revealed for many in the region elements of their past from the perspective of an observer who had a foot in both the long-ago and the here-and-now.

Southwest Georgians became eager to read each new accounting, to get a first-hand report from their man on the mule wagon. And even when he decided to leave that newest adventure to others and prepare for a going-away that would leave his many admirers mourning "the loss of a vital part of us," Doug had a few more gifts left in his bag of tricks, poignant tales of a past that made him the man he became.

The stories herein are a wonder, a collection of anecdotes that will leave you at times chuckling at the misdeeds in the southwest Georgia woods and at times with a tear or two in your eyes at the tender connection of this man and his element. Yes, Doug Porter is an essential figure to the people of southwest Georgia. Enjoy his stories. He'll become one for you as well.

Carlton Fletcher, Editor
The Albany Herald

Introduction

When I lived there, Albany, Georgia billed itself as "The Good Life City." It was a Flint River community located in the heart of the Deep South—surrounded by cotton fields, peanut farms, and quail hunting plantations. A place where we smiled at strangers, hugged our friends, and talked kind of slow. I moved there in 2004 to become the Executive Director of a 700-acre park and twelve years later I retired after a forty-year career managing parks, zoos, and museums.

But like many retirees, I wasn't ready to sit around all day. So, I landed a part-time job to keep me busy. It was a job that kept me in contact with animals, but in a manner with which I had little experience—driving a mule wagon at a high-end, exclusive quail hunting plantation. It was, in fact, a job that is something of a lost art and which people find fascinating. It launched yet a third career writing about it for my local newspaper, the *Albany Herald*.

My articles included some reflections on quail hunting with the "rich and famous" as viewed from the driver's seat of the wagon. Eventually, I attempted to unpack some of the baggage of modern, South Georgia plantation culture. But sitting on that wagon also gave me time to reflect on other aspects of my life. I wrote about the natural world, my southern family roots, and the gnomes that may (or may not) have lived in my garden. I contributed articles about hunting dogs, therapy dogs, herding dogs, racing dogs, and war dogs.

Since that first article in 2017, I contributed about sixty pieces to the *Herald* before I retired from the wagon, moved to Atlanta, and sent-in my final dispatch as a "foreign correspondent" in June of 2022. I even wrote a few books along the way including a novel, *The Dogcatcher and The Fox*, and a memoir, *Lessons from the Zoo: Ten Animals That Changed My Life*.

But it all began with those articles about a couple of mules named Thelma and Louise and a hunting dog named Joy.

1

Giddy Up, Mule

Originally Published March 8, 2017

If you want to gain an appreciation for the conveniences of modern transportation, try driving a team of mules for a few months. I became a mule aficionado after driving a wagon at a local quail hunting plantation, but I also came to appreciate where the term "stubborn as a mule" comes from. I was grateful that they were not my primary means of transport.

In their heyday, mules were as common as automobiles are today. As a young boy, my dad plowed his family farm behind a mule. Twenty-mule teams hauled tons of borax out of Death Valley, California. Mules dragged cannons across the Western Front in WWI and served as pack animals in the WWII Burma Campaign. On the home front, mules pulled wagons and farm implements up until the 1930s, when they were replaced by tractors and trucks.

Mule barns, like the mule barn in downtown Albany, Georgia, were combination gas stations, garages, and hardware stores, dealing in mules, horses, and all types of transportation supplies. In 1911, according to Mary Braswell's Looking Back column in the January 8th, 2017, *Albany Herald*, "J. J. Battle of Battle Brothers (mules and horses) brought from Tennessee a trainload of mules including two carloads of heavy road mules, turpentine mules and others adapted to all classes of heavy work."

As a part-time wagon driver, I spent many hours holding the reins and staring at the fine, muscular behinds of two mules that I affectionately called Thelma and Louise. Their radar-like ears were usually turned back toward me, listening for a "giddy up" or a "whoa mule." They pulled me up hills and through mud holes. They went impossibly slow when heading out to hunt in the mornings but returned to the barn at the end of the day at a brisk trot—if not a dead-run. They learned to whoa when I said "whoa," but insisted on backing up when I wanted them to stand still—until I found a stick that was long enough to poke them in the behind. The left side of the wagon-tongue was always slightly ahead of the right side as Thelma did most of the work while Louise nipped at her side, trying to get her to slow down. Louise was the one that tried to kick me when I groomed her in the morning.

When hunting season was over, my mules spent the next seven months eating grass and rolling in the dust in their pasture with the other mules and horses. I wonder if they missed me—missed the oat and apple treats I slipped them in the mornings, missed pulling the wagon across the fields as the dogs ran around and beneath them and the horses grazed in front of them, missed the people laughing and talking while shotguns boomed in the distance. Probably not. But I sure missed them as I looked forward to next season—although this quote from the pen of William Faulkner did give me pause: "A mule will labor ten years willingly and patiently for you, for the privilege of kicking you once."

2

A Peaceful Pace

Published December 17, 2017

Being the driver of a mule-drawn wagon on a quail hunting plantation afforded me plenty of time to think. Sometimes my thoughts were directed toward the job at hand—the mules, the horses, the dogs, and the hunters—and sometimes my thoughts were drawn to the conversations behind me on the wagon—conversations that I treated as confidential. And then there were the long periods of quiet that reminded me of the quote often attributed to *Winnie the Pooh* author, A.A. Milne: "Sometimes I sits and thinks, and sometimes I just sits...."

At the end of every hunt, we had a fifteen- or twenty-minute ride back to the big-house. The dogs were back in the wagon and the retriever was lying on the seat beside me as I followed the horse riders. The only sound was the conversation of the guests, the jingle of the mule harnesses, and the occasional bobwhite quail whistling in the tall grass. The pace was slow enough for a person to walk and I never heard a guest complain about the length of our ride. In fact, people often remarked on how peaceful it was and how they could feel their blood pressure going down.

Our wagon was like an old-fashioned covered wagon with its heavy wooden body and tall, spoked (albeit rubber-tired) wheels. It was not a stretch to imagine a time when this type of transportation was the norm. My Grandma Porter told me of her trip from the Florida panhandle to Nacogdoches, Texas on a covered wagon in the late 1800s—a trip of about six hundred miles. According to Google Maps, I could drive that trip in just under ten hours. My grandma's journey, at about three miles an hour, would probably have taken several months.

I wondered what it would be like for me to drive to work in the mornings on my wagon. I would not need to worry about running into deer or hogs. I wouldn't be checking my speedometer or gas gauge. Of course, the drive would last about three hours instead of fifteen minutes. It would be like commuting from Albany to Atlanta—with no iTunes or satellite radio. With all that time, I could have solved a lot of the world's problems.

The people who hunted with us were busy people. They spent plenty of time on their mobile phones making deals and staying in touch with their offices. I even had one guest suggest that we make the wagon a "mobile hotspot" so he would have better phone reception. But on the ride to the house at the end of the day, all that seemed to change. The phones stayed in their pockets as their conversations steered away from business and toward family, good times, and the beauty that surrounded them.

In his *Zen Habits* blog, author Leo Babauta offers us "Ten Essential Rules for Slowing Down and Enjoying Life More." The first five are to do less, to be present, to disconnect, to focus on people, and to appreciate nature. That about covers the experience of spending the day on a mule wagon. It certainly gave me time to think about such things as how the dog handler controlled the pointers with a whistle and a "whoa," why the retrievers raced out to find a quail with such enthusiasm, and what—if anything—the mules were thinking about as they stood immobile awaiting my command to "giddy-up." I'll let you know when I work out some answers. In the meantime, I think I'll "just sits."

3

Working on Mule Time

Published December 31, 2017

My mules stood patiently in front of the wagon for hours every day with eyes forward, but ears turned back awaiting my instructions. They would move a little and stop as the quail hunters moved through the woods, all the while appearing oblivious to the shotgun blasts and the skittering dogs that ran beneath them. All I needed to do was rattle the reins and say a gentle "giddy up" for them to move and utter a "whoa" with a tug on the reins for them to stop. It all worked like a machine until about four o'clock every afternoon. That was when Louise, the right-side mule, began to act up whenever we stopped. It started with the toss of her head, progressed to the stomp of a foot, and culminated when she reached over and tried to bite her partner, Thelma, on the neck. Thelma reacted by squealing and moving away—something that was difficult while harnessed to the wagon. I reached forward and flicked Louise on the rump with my modified fishing rod and said a loud "Quit." Both mules would then stand still for a while, but after less than a minute Louise tossed her head, and the process began again.

I loved my mules, but not in the late afternoon when I recalled the thoughts of Harry S. Truman, who apparently knew a thing or two about mules when he said: "My favorite animal is the mule. He has more horse sense than a horse. He knows when to stop eating – and he knows when to stop working." We were supposed to stop working every day at about 4:45 so we could take our guests back to the big-house for dinner. Louise, it appeared, was on a different clock. She wanted to stop working on her own time—which was apparently at about four o'clock.

Thelma and Louise were a couple of beautiful blondes with long ears, large rumps, and oversized personalities. Thelma stood stoically every morning while I placed her harness. Louise, on the other hand, would occasionally lift a hind hoof as I was brushing her and threaten to kick me into next week. There may be nothing to be learned from the second kick of a mule, as Mark Twain suggested, but I did my best not to receive my first one.

When they were in-harness and ready to pull and I gave the command to "giddy up," Louise jerked forward to get the wagon started and that was the only work she did all day. The rest of the time, it was Thelma's harness that was taut from pulling and it was Thelma that arrived back at the barn at the end of the day covered in sweat. Louise was as fresh as a vine-ripened tomato—no sweat, no heavy breathing, and eager to get out to the pasture for her evening graze.

Thelma and Louise were about seventeen years old, which put them in their prime in mule years. The mules on the other wagon were each twenty-seven and, with a life expectancy of thirty years or more, were nearing the end of their wagon-pulling days. That is why we needed to break in some new mules—a couple of light gray, short-haired, seven-year-old males I called Bert and Ernie.

When they were pulling the wagon, Bert worked on my left and was the steady one—much like Thelma. Ernie, on the other hand, was skittish. He refused to walk through the wagon shed where we parked the wagons at the end of the day. When I attempted to drive through the open shed so I could park the wagon, he suspiciously eyeballed the coiled hose, the garbage can, and the pallet of supplies on our right side and he eased to his left pushing Bert out of line. I was forced to stop the wagon and have someone pull the mules forward and into position. One evening as we were driving in at the end of the day, we encountered a basketball-sized pile of Spanish moss lying in the middle of the road. The horses stepped over it without hesitation, but Ernie saw it before I did and tilted his head, looking at it nervously. The nearer we got, the higher he raised his head until he began to push Bert to the left into the tall grass at the edge of the road. No amount of pressure on the reins could pull them back in line. Thankfully there were no trees or ditches in our new path, and I was able to wrangle them back into the road when the "danger" was safely passed.

Bert and Ernie came in at different times, so they were not a pair of pulling mules that had been trained to work together. That was most evident when I asked them to "giddy up" and they pulled sideways in different directions. If I was not careful, they would even begin to back up. Eventually, after a lot of persuasion on my part, one of them would jerk forward and another uncertain journey began.

I viewed us as a team, my mules and me, with the three of us doing our part. I needed them to pull the wagon as much as they needed me to guide them. I got paid to drive a wagon and they also got paid—in food, water, safety, and a life more at ease in the pasture than occasionally pulling a wagon.

When all was going well, I suppose driving a mule wagon looked effortless as we glided peacefully through the fields. But there were times when I wondered if Oliver Wendell Holmes, Jr. had me in mind when he quipped, "You will never appreciate the potentialities of the English language until you have heard a southern mule driver search the soul of a mule."

With Louise and the new boys, I certainly used some colorful language when searching the soul of my mules—if there was a soul to search.

4

The View from a Wagon: As Natural as Life

Published January 31, 2018

Many of us, it seems, are disconnected from the source of our food. Deep down we know that if we eat meat, some animal had to provide that meat—but it is not something to be talked about in polite society.

This was illustrated when my wife, an elementary school librarian, was speaking to a first-grade class after reading a story about what animals eat. She explained the differences among carnivores, herbivores, and omnivores but when asked what category humans fall into, the students became confused. Many did not realize that humans eat other animals—that when eating hamburger, they are eating a cow, or when consuming bacon they are eating a pig. This urban generation is being raised on shrink-wrapped food from the grocery store. I wondered if some parents might be upset that their children were being told otherwise.

Why the disconnect? Perhaps it is because we don't want to think about the fact that animals are killed to supply our meat. We are content with the store-bought illusion. This reminds me of the story (probably untrue, but a good story nonetheless) about a display presented by showman P. T. Barnum early in his career. It was called *The Happy Family*, and it is said to have featured a lion, a tiger, a panther, and a lamb—all in the same cage. After the exhibition had been running for a while, a friend asked the showman how everything was going. "Oh, fairly well," Barnum replied. "I'm going to make a permanent feature out of it, if the supply of lambs holds out."

The guests I met when I drove the wagon were, for the most part, enthusiastic sportsmen. They loved shooting the way some people love golf, even to the point of cheering the well-placed shot. Most of them were more like me than I ever suspected. They were naturalists at heart. They may have flown in on private jets and carried shotguns that cost more than a new car, but they still marveled at the vultures that soared overhead, asked about the prescribed fire that maintains quail habitat, and got excited when a Cooper's hawk swooped in to steal one of their birds. They were as knowledgeable about what quail eat as they were what size shotgun shell will bring them down and they believed in giving the birds a sporting chance to get away. Most would not shoot unless their target was well into the air and flapping madly in the opposite direction.

I am not a hunter. It's not that I disapprove; it's just that shooting guns and killing animals is not my thing. I have, however, seen lions in Africa kill an antelope. It is a different experience in person than it is on television. It is more visceral, more intense, and it helped me realize that it is perfectly natural for one animal to die in order to feed another.

It is more than a little ironic that in my retirement after a career in zoos, where our goal was to extend the lives of animals, I found myself part of an operation that harvested (a polite euphemism for kills) hundreds of quail every month. My justification—if any is needed—is that death is as natural as life itself. The birds that were killed in our operation were dropped into a box on the wagon and placed on ice after each hunt. They were then cleaned, packaged, and frozen—ready for consumption by our guests. They were harvested at least as humanely as the billions of chickens who are slaughtered every year to provide our chicken nuggets, wings, and fingers.

Author Temple Grandin uses her autism and her expertise as an animal science professor at Colorado State University as a platform to advocate for the humane treatment of the livestock we slaughter for food. In her 2009 book *Animals Make Us Human*, she suggests that our relationship with the animals we use for food should be humane and even mutually beneficial. If we are going to take animals for food, then we should provide those animals with a good quality of life prior to that use. Her premise is that it is okay for humans to eat meat as long as our relationship with the animals we eat is humane.

I often wondered as I sat on my wagon and watched the hunters stalk the broomsedge and wiregrass hoping to flush another covey what that landscape would look like without quail hunters paying for its preservation. My guess is that the wide open, pine-wiregrass habitat would be swallowed up in a scrub oak forest. The quail, gopher tortoise, and other savanna-loving creatures would disappear. Perhaps the people who oppose hunting as cruel and barbaric might see the end of hunting as a victory but, from where I sat on the wagon, it would be a hollow victory indeed.

5

Off the Beaten Path

Published May 9, 2018

There's one in every crowd—even a crowd of mules. I'm talking about that individual who marches to her own drummer—who says: *I will not follow where the path may lead, but I will go where there is no path, and I will leave a trail.*

I witnessed such an individual at the quail hunting plantation where I drove a wagon. The occasion was the annual meeting of the Georgia chapter of the Colonial Dames of America. The event was a historic preservation tour that brought them to view the house designed by world famous architect, Edward Vason Jones.

It is worth noting that when hunting season ended on the last day of February, the animals took the summer off while the property managers were hard at work burning fields, clearing brush, and maintaining equipment. Since it was a private residence and a members-only facility, nobody came on the property unless they had business there. When I arrived on the property that day, the horses and mules were grazing peacefully in their fifty-acre pasture—peacefully, that is, until three large white tour busses followed by a small caravan of cars trundled down the dirt road in front of their pasture.

I can only imagine what was going through their minds as the vehicles disgorged a hundred or so passengers. Maybe they thought all these people had come to see them—perhaps bringing food. It was quite a sight to see six mules and a dozen horses sprinting across the pasture to gather along the white wooden fence. It reminded me of when I was a kid, and we heard the bells of the ice cream truck jingling through the neighborhood.

I paid little attention, assuming the guests would lose interest in a bunch of animals in favor of the historic house they had come to see. Imagine my surprise when I looked back and discovered that they had gathered around one of the mules who was grazing peacefully in the middle of the lawn. How had that happened? Had she jumped the fence? Not likely. Had someone left the gate open? Not according to a quick survey of the fence line.

The mule was one of the mules that pulled my wagon, my dependable pulling mule, Thelma. She gave me little trouble as I herded her back up the lane and through a gate that led back to the pasture. She even seemed—if I care to be anthropomorphic—glad to see me.

So, how did she get out? Well, that's the interesting bit. According to several guests who witnessed it, when the other animals were trotting to the fence, Thelma separated herself and turned ninety degrees from the herd. She proceeded with purpose down the fence line away from the action and entered a grove of trees where the sturdy wooden fence became a tangle of metal posts and barbed wire—a section of fence that was apparently less than secure. Guests reported that when she emerged from the trees she was no longer in the pasture. She had decided to join the party.

How, I wonder, did she figure that out? How did she have the presence of mind to zig when the rest of the herd zagged? I can't say, but it sure did make for some good theater. I wonder what made the greater impression on our guests from around the state, the architecture of Edward Vason Jones or the ingenuity of Thelma the wayward mule, who challenged us not to "follow where the path may lead, but to go where there is no path and leave a trail."

6

Shotguns: Tools of the Trade

Published February 2, 2019

As the driver of a mule wagon at a quail hunting plantation, I probably handed out more shotgun shells than some gun store owners. I kept it in a compartment on the wagon at my feet—mostly 20 gauge and 28 gauge. Most people used 20-gauge shells since they carry a slightly larger load. Counter intuitively, the smaller the number, the larger the size of the shot in the shell. I kept a box of 12-gauge shells but never had anyone ask for them. They are too large and powerful to use on the quail. I also kept a few boxes of slender 410 shells, which carry a much smaller load and seem to be for the serious, more skilled shooters.

Most people used a double-barreled, over and under shotgun that breaks down to load. Their guns rested in a wagon box for the hunters who rode with me and in saddle scabbards for the horseback riders. I didn't handle the guns, so they were a bit of a mystery to me. But when you are around them as much as I was you can't help but draw some conclusions.

One observation is that shotguns aren't really guns—not like *we-need-to-get-guns-off-the-street* guns. They are tools. They can be works of art. Some are family heirlooms, passed down from generation to generation. To the serious hunter, a shotgun is more than just a gun.

If you search for shotguns at the big sporting goods retailers, they will range in price from a few hundred dollars up to several thousand. I overheard a conversation between two hunters in which they discussed a shotgun worth $30,000, so I went online to see what they might be talking about.

Perhaps they were discussing a shotgun produced by the English gun maker James Purdey & Sons, a company that has been supplying guns to royalty, aristocrats, and the wealthy since 1814. The price for a Purdey, considered by many to be the ultimate in shotguns, is around $30,000 with a delivery time of over two years. They are, of course, "lovingly built by hand." But if you're going all-in on your shotgun, another British gun-maker offers the Holland & Holland Royal Deluxe shotgun, available for well over $200,000.

In addition to the guns, I also came to appreciate the art of shooting—especially with the break-down double-barreled gun. Two shots, that's all you get. Shoot, break, eject, reload, and shoot. It was like an exquisitely choreographed dance. I saw it a thousand times, and it never got old. I loved the thrill of a double (when a person hit a bird with each of his two shots). Even more special was when someone hit two birds with one shot—probably just luck, but fun to watch, nonetheless. Once in a while we would host a guy who hunted with a 410 shotgun. Some of those guys knocked down bird after bird. For them, shooting quail looked like instinct not aim.

The other extreme was the novice hunter who endured miss after miss. I never laughed at those guys since I couldn't hit the side of a barn if I was standing inside it. I always felt for the novice. He was nervous. The experienced hunter would grab his ammo before we left the house in the morning and was always armed and ready to go. The novice hunter was often like the person in the checkout line at the grocery store who digs around in her purse looking for her checkbook after the cashier has rung up her groceries. This was the guy who waited until the dogs were on point, and everyone had dismounted to hunt before he patted his vest pockets and realized he needed something to put in his gun. The inexperienced hunter may not hit a bird all day, but if he did, when he made his first kill, everyone—even the wagon driver—cheered.

A final observation about the guns we used for quail hunting is how they sounded. There was a distinctive bang that all of us—horses, mules, dogs, and people—were used to. The hunters were often too far from the wagon for me to see what they were shooting at, but with two hunters and two shells in each gun, I could count the shots—one, two, three, four. Any fewer meant someone failed to get off a shot. Perhaps he forgot to turn off the safety or waited until the birds were too far away.

I also learned that there was a different kind of bang, a much louder one. This was the sound of a hunter who had turned too far—the sound of a gun aimed in my direction. I couldn't help but try to duck even though, from my perch on the wagon seat, I was the highest target for miles around. Fortunately, nobody ever came close to hitting me, but if they did, some poor nurse was going to be digging a bucket-full of birdshot out of my backside.

7

Southerners Tend to Slow Life Down

Published September 15, 2018

I went to the plantation a few mornings one September to take a couple of mules out for some test drives before hunting season began. Bert and Ernie hadn't been very well behaved when pulling the wagon and I wanted us (the mules and me) to get in a bit of practice before we had guests onboard. The season before had been no fun pulling up to the big house with a couple of wide-eyed, skittish mules that refused to stand still and, when they took off, pulled in different directions. When we were loading guests for the morning hunt, I was supposed to be the expert muleskinner, so it was a little embarrassing when I couldn't control my mules.

As it turned out, the mules were fine. The only hiccup on our practice run was when we came to a dip in the road that was filled with water. Ernie, we discovered, would not walk through water and no amount of hollering and shaking the reins was going to persuade him otherwise. Instead, he pulled hard to the left and jammed one of the wheels against a tree causing some anxious moments as the front left wheel climbed the buttress root of the tree, threatening to turn the wagon over. Luckily, the mules stopped, and we were able to get them unhitched and move the wagon into a position that would allow them to skirt the waterhole. Better to find out the problem before we had guests onboard.

This made me think about what was involved in providing guests with a great experience in the name of southern hospitality. When the wagon arrived at the big house in the morning to load guests and guns, it was handshakes all around as we introduced ourselves with smiles and laughter. We humans do love our rituals. If we were dogs, we'd be wagging our tails and smelling each other's butts.

As host of the guests on my wagon, I tried to cheerfully provide for their needs—water and soft drinks in the cooler and plenty of ammunition in the box at my feet. If it was cold, I'd have blankets and coffee. If rain was in the forecast, I'd have rain gear available. As we were moving about the property, I tried to maintain the right balance of respectful silence and cheerful banter. My goal was to be a good host—to provide hospitality or, in our case, *southern hospitality*.

Southern hospitality is an institution that, according to humorist Roy Blount, Jr., goes back to the days before air conditioning. When folks showed up at your house, Blount suggests, you couldn't pretend you weren't home when there you were, sitting on the porch. You could pretend to be dead, he says, but then you couldn't fan yourself.

I was born and raised in the South where children are taught that when they say yes or no to a grown-up, it had better be followed by a Sir or a Ma'am. My family's roots go back generations. So, it should not have come as a surprise when, after a decade and a half living in the North, I moved back to Georgia and people seemed so friendly. When I passed strangers on the street, they would actually make eye contact and say hello. Acquaintances would see me in the grocery store and stop to ask about my family. And, after I got to know someone a little better, I needed to be ready for a hug when I saw them. People can claim what they want about race relations in the South, but this old white guy has had some of the world's best hugs from my African American lady friends.

The late southern journalist Lewis Grizzard said that "Yankees still ain't real sure how smart we are. When I lived in Chicago," Grizzard said, "people used to ask, 'Do you people read?'."

I believe that is because life in the South tends to move at a slower pace than other parts of the world. We talk real slow, we walk real slow, and we even think real slow. Maybe that's the secret to southern hospitality. When we're moving slowly, we can take the time to focus on other people.

Being a wagon driver forced me into intimate contact with a variety of people. One of the tricks I learned from my experience was that being nice often resulted in people being nice back. The wagon made for a very pleasant way to slow life down and focus on those around us.

Zimbabwean author Alexander McCall Smith in his book *The Double Comfort Safari Club* had his character Precious Ramotswe say that her father had taught her everything she knew about how to lead a good life. "Don't complain" was her father's motto. He told her not to blame others for things that she brought on herself, to be content with who she is, and to do whatever she can to bring to others such contentment, and joy, and understanding that she has managed to find herself. Perhaps that is the secret to southern hospitality—bringing contentment, joy, and understanding to others—and doing it *real slow*.

8

Standing Up for What's Right

Published August 18, 2017

I grew up in the segregated South to a poor family—but a family favored with what has come to be known as *the power of whiteness*. My dad's family goes back generations in south Alabama and the Florida panhandle. They probably even owned slaves. But I can't turn back the clock and undo the past. Slavery was an abomination that ended in the United States 150 years ago. What really makes me sad is that we southern whites found a way to keep slavery alive for another hundred years. I saw the evidence with my own eyes. I remember the "colored" restrooms and drinking fountains, and the "white only" waiting rooms and country clubs. It makes me uncomfortable to remember that it took heroic effort and bravery for African Americans to earn the rights that a free people should have had all along. So, what heritage am I as a white, southerner allowed to be proud of?

I am proud of the people, both black and white, of my generation and older who are able to put all of that behind them and work together in friendship and brotherly love. I am proud of a southern heritage of politeness where we say hello to strangers on the street and we teach our youngsters to say "Yes Ma'am" and "No Sir" to their elders. I love it that we make northerners uncomfortable when we move in for a hug. And I am proud of my parents who in the 1970s, when the schools in St. Petersburg, Florida were integrating, sent my younger brother to a high school that had been all-black for generations. While the rest of the white community was huffing in indignation, my parents had the courage to stand up to the white flight that caused others to flee to the suburbs. My brother, David, was an athlete who excelled at football and basketball. He was the only white player on the football and basketball teams his junior year. That meant my parents were the only white faces in the stands.

I can be proud of my southern heritage, without being proud of everything my ancestors did. But my southern heritage is complicated. It is a heritage of white folks versus black folks, and a heritage of southern gentility alongside the ugliness of racism. I can't change who I am – a white, southern, male – and I can't change the past, but I don't need a Confederate battle flag or the statue of a Confederate general to remind me of who I am.

I know there are plenty of good, decent white people who are appalled by the message of the neo-Nazis and white supremacists. But this issue is not going to be resolved by more marches and sit-ins by people of color alone. This particular brand of evil also needs to be squashed by white people standing up to other white people and telling them they don't speak for us. As for me, I'll write about it. I'll shout about it. And, if need be, I'll stand up against those who preach hatred. It just makes me sad that nearly fifty years after the death of Martin Luther King we are still having this conversation. "Make America Great Again" rings kind of hollow right about now.

9

An Ode to Joy

Published January 17, 2018

A quail hunt, at least on the property where I worked, was filled with pageantry. We arrived under the ancient live-oaks at the big house at precisely nine o'clock in the morning—two mule-drawn wagons with six or eight horses led by hunting guides in white vests. It was such an impressive sight that first time guests often stood on the porch and recorded the procession with their cell phones.

In all this pageantry—mules, horses, wagons, and guides—one individual was often singled out. She stood on the seat of the first wagon, as she had done for nearly a decade, and was clearly the star of the show. She was a thirty-pound, chocolate brown English cocker named Joy.

To say I love dogs would be an understatement. Dogs have been a part of my life since the day I was born. My childhood dogs were yard-dogs that never came in the house but in those days, children seldom went in the house either, except to eat or sleep. Dogs ran with us—or we ran with them.

In my adult life, my wife and I have always shared our home with one or two dogs as part of the family, and I still grieve for the ones that have passed. Maybe that is why I had such an affinity for the dogs in our hunting operation and why I loved spending my workday with Joy on my lap.

Every morning, after we loaded guests and guns and we rode out to the hunting ground, the first order of business was to stop the wagon and get two dogs down. They were English pointers, muscular little short-haired dogs with names like Buck and Gabby, Bud and Pearl, and Ike and Dot.

They were taken out of the wagon in a male-female pair and positioned side by side in the middle of the road, with a gentle tug on their collars and an equally gentle command to "whoa." The control of the dog handler was impressive and must have been the result of hours, weeks, and even years of training. The dogs stood still and looked at their handler as he mounted his horse, listening for their release—a low whistle, not unlike the whistle of the bobwhite quail.

Once released, they ran up and down the dirt roads and in and out of the grassy lanes. By all outward appearances, they were running aimlessly at a brisk trot—aimlessly, that is, until one of them caught the scent of quail in the thick grass. Then it looked like the dog had come to the end of some invisible leash. His head snapped toward the birds and his body jerked sideways. He remained immobile with head down and tail up. Our guide said, "We've got a point up here." The other dog was usually not nearby but when she saw a point, she would also fall into a less serious point, essentially honoring her partner.

It was a bit of a mystery to me, especially from my vantage point on the wagon, how the dog handler interpreted the actions of the dogs. Was the dog pointing to a covey or a single bird or a bird that was the morning meal for a hawk? Were both dogs on the same covey or were there in fact two coveys? This was the heart of the hunt—the dogs on point and the guide positioning the hunters; followed by the moment of truth when the birds flew, the guns boomed, and the birds fell. This was when Joy, the little English cocker on the wagon seat next to me, stopped whining and jumping around. She stood at full-alert, remaining silent while awaiting the dog handler's call.

Most of the birds fell in an open area where they were easily picked up. Occasionally, however, a bird fell into the deep grass. That took a little more looking, even when the hunter knew where his bird fell. After a few moments of fruitless searching, the call went up from the guide as he looked back to the wagon and hollered, "JOY!"

Joy scrambled down the steps at the side of the wagon and navigated the lanes to where the hunters and guides waited. The guide pointed and said, "dead bird in here," and Joy went to work. She scrambled back and forth, nose to the ground in ever shrinking circles, until she homed in on her target. Finally, she dove in and emerged with a bird in her mouth. She looked to the guide who said "wagon," and back she came to deliver the bird to me and turn her attention back to the action in the field.

This was clearly a highlight for the hunters and was the reason that after ten seasons Joy was, at least on our wagon, the star of the show. She was the enthusiastic magician pulling an invisible bird out of the deep grass and bounding back to the wagon with her treasure. That, I suppose, is why Joy was the first one the hunters greeted when they came out on the porch of the house in the morning and the last one to be touched with an affectionate pat on the head before they went inside for drinks after the hunt.

There is a tendency for people unfamiliar with their lives to feel sorry for the dogs on a hunting plantation. They live in a kennel and only come out to train or to hunt. But not all dogs are bred to live in a house and sleep on a couch. Many were bred to guard property, pull sleds, or perform water rescue. The Jack Russell terrier, for example, is described as a "charming and affectionate" little dog, but it was developed in England over two hundred years ago for the not-so-charming job of hunting foxes. The hunting dogs I worked with were bred to find, to point, and to retrieve birds. I didn't think Joy's life would be better or she would be any "happier" if she retired to someone's house to never seek out another quail in the deep grass.

When the hunters came out in the morning and came directly to the wagon to rub Joy's head, it was as if she was their talisman—a good luck charm that might hold magical properties. But if, as John Milton has suggested, "luck is the residue of design," then luck would have little to do with the success of the day's hunt. The pointers would point the birds and Joy would retrieve them—that much was certain. It was the skill of the hunters that was a little less certain. They would need to rely on quick reactions and straight shooting rather than the luck derived from petting their "lucky dog." And no one would be happier with their success than Joy, as she lived out her name and trotted out to help them find their lost birds.

10

The Dog's Nose Knows

Published March 26, 2021

Dogs "see" the world through their noses. My first direct experience with this almost mystical ability came early in my zoo career. Those were the days when my wife insisted that I disrobe in the laundry room and jump in the shower when I got home from work. It was not because of some unknown contagion, as with today's medical professionals. It was because—not to put too fine a point on it—I often stank.

One evening when I was leaning against the washing machine, exhausted from a day of manhandling a herd of antelope for a medical procedure, my dog Simba—a big brown rescue dog of unknown lineage—wandered in wagging her stump of a tail. She licked me on the hand, sniffed my leg, and snarled at my pants as she jumped back barking. Simba was warning me of unseen danger in our midst.

For humans, smell is often considered our least important sense. I didn't smell anything on this particular evening, but Simba sure did. After nearly half a century of working with animals in zoos, I have become desensitized to smells. During my career, I shoveled wheelbarrows full of elephant poop, hosed urine-soaked tiger cages, and had angry chimpanzees splatter me with their feces. After a while, I just learned to turn off my smeller. My wife also overcame her aversion to animal aromas. She helped foster a baby gorilla when I was deputy director of the Toledo Zoo and thirty years later, she still remembers the strong, earthy, old-fruit smell of the gorillas.

It was, I suppose, not that difficult for me to block certain smells since the human sense of smell is somewhat rudimentary. The inside of our nose is lined with specialized tissue which can receive air-born molecules that our brains process as scents. The tissue inside a human nose is covered with five or six million receptor sites, all clustered in one spot at the back of our nasal cavity. That might sound impressive until we consider that a dog's nose has forty times as many receptors—two or three-hundred million. They line the entire internal surface of the dog's nose from the nostrils to the back of the throat. In addition, the dog's brain devotes much more capacity to processing those smells. The smell experience for a dog is exponentially more acute than ours. Simba had never seen an antelope, but she knew that whatever she smelled on my pants did not belong in her house.

We humans have recognized the power of a dog's nose for millennia. A third-century scholar, for example, mentions "a hound of unrivaled scenting powers, so intensely devoted to his work that he could not be pulled off the trail until his quarry was found." Perhaps this was an early version of the modern bloodhound.

According to the American Kennel Club, bloodhounds as we know them were perfected in western Europe about a thousand years ago. During the centuries since, they have earned a reputation as trackers without equal. Police departments around the world have relied on bloodhounds to follow the scent of criminals, lost children, and confused seniors. But we have come to learn that the dog's ability to identify a scent may be less about the breed and more about desire and training. Dogs can not only sniff out quail in deep grass or follow the days-old trail of an escaped outlaw. Dogs can also be trained to detect drugs, explosives, and even cancer.

Science tells us that a scent is a chemical particle that floats in through the nose and is processed into a form that's readable by the brain. Brain cells then carry that information to the amygdala—the same area of the brain that processes emotions—before taking it to the adjoining hippocampus, where learning and memory formation take place.

Scents are the only sensations that travel a direct path to the emotional and memory centers of the brain. That results in an intimate connection between emotions, memories, and scents. Perhaps that is why we can use specific scents to sell. Realtors have suggested sellers bake cookies just before a home showing. Bakeries have been known to exhaust the smell of cinnamon buns baking in the oven to entice customers into the store. And this is why memories triggered by scents (as opposed to other senses) are experienced as more emotional and more evocative. A familiar but long-forgotten scent can even bring people to tears.

When I worked with elephants, I discovered a scent so strong that I brought it home infused into my clothing and hair. Even a long, hot shower sometimes failed to rinse it off. Elephant smell was best described by John M. Kelley, of the Ringling Bros. and Barnum & Bailey Circus when he said:

"You cannot see it or feel it, yet it clings like a mother's love. Its vaporized essence is so real that you cannot dilute it, dissolve it, liquify it, freeze it, smother it, counterfeit it, cut it, shake it, or lose it. Elephant smell is the fourth dimension."

When I am driving the mule wagon on a quail hunt, my passengers spend the day watching dogs use their sensitive noses to sniff out tiny birds in acres of deep grass. In contrast, when the mules a few feet in front of us defecate, the pungent, earthy smell barely registers with we humans. It is the sight of what they are doing, not the smell, that causes us to recoil. But let an over-excited hunting dog poop in the wagon box behind us and our threshold for smelling kicks into high gear. That's a "vaporized essence" that triggers some evocative emotions—emotions that have all of us on the wagon ready to abandon ship.

11

Diggory the Greyhound: Canine Royalty

Published February 28, 2021

Have you ever been at some event or gathering when someone walked in and took over the room? Perhaps it was the host, or the guest of honor, or maybe a well-known celebrity. But the moment they walk in, the electricity changes. Conversations slow, eyes turn, the air seems to get sucked out of the room. I have seen it with people on numerous occasions, but the day I met Diggory was the first time with a dog.

He came into my son's living room from the basement apartment where he lived with his owner, Will. His arrival was unexpected. The door to the basement opened and there he was, striding confidently—majestic and regal—into the room. Diggory was a fawn colored, seventy-five pound, three-foot-tall greyhound. I was nearest the door sitting at the kitchen table, so he came to me first, gazed at me across the table, sniffed my arm, and moved on. He checked both humans and dogs as he circled the room, moving with the easy fluid grace of an elite athlete. He finally curled up on an impossibly small dog bed in the corner.

From the moment I saw Diggory, I could see why greyhounds are such special creatures. Diggory was the essence of the dog breeder's credo "form follows function." From his sleek aerodynamic head to his broad chest that curves into a tightly tucked waist, his smooth hide was stretched over muscle and bone without an ounce of fat.

Greyhounds have been an object of fascination for artists, poets, and kings for as long as human beings have been civilized. Legend has it that Cleopatra had coursing greyhounds and greyhounds were the hunting hounds of ancient mythical gods and goddesses. Over the centuries, greyhounds have traveled with explorers and generals, adorned the suites of kings and queens, and appeared in fine art and literature.

According to the American Kennel Club (AKC), greyhounds belong in the Hound Group—a diverse lot that defies generalization. Hounds can be long low dachshunds or Irish wolfhounds, the AKC's tallest breed. The group includes elkhounds, coonhounds, deerhounds, Afghans, and beagles. Most hounds share the common ancestral trait of being used for hunting. Some use an acute sense of smell to follow a trail. Others demonstrate a phenomenal gift of stamina as they relentlessly run down quarry. And then there is the blinding speed of the greyhound.

Greyhounds were bred for hunting in the open where their pursuit speed and keen eyesight were essential. The original use of greyhounds was in running down smaller animals for meat. Later, they became specialized in competition hare coursing. Some greyhounds are still used for coursing in artificial lure sports like dog racing. Before he retired, Diggory was a racer. He ran under the name Mega Diggory and some of his races can still be seen on the internet.

My connection with greyhound racing is etched in vivid childhood memories. My dad was a plasterer who had a second job to help support our family. On weekends and Wednesday evenings he worked as an assistant starter at Derby Lane dog track in St. Petersburg, Florida.

Derby Lane, the St. Petersburg Kennel Club, claimed to be the oldest continuously operating greyhound track in the world. It was carved out of palmetto scrubland on the edge of Tampa Bay in the 1920s. The club's first race was held on the afternoon of January 3, 1925. The final race was nearly a century later in December 2020, just days before greyhound racing was banned in Florida. According to the Humane Society of the United States, greyhound racing is cruel and inhumane and is now illegal in more than forty states, including Florida.

I wasn't allowed to attend the regular dog races because Derby Lane was a gambling establishment—no children allowed—but I did go to the schooling races on occasion. These were practice races, probably for young dogs, and I never observed anything cruel or inhumane.

The starting box, where my dad worked, consisted of a long, low unit with eight greyhound sized stalls. The handlers walked the dogs to the box on a leash and my dad helped them remove the leash and stuff dogs in the box. Each dog wore a colorful vest with a number from one to eight on it. Once the dogs were loaded, a mechanical arm was activated and a fuzzy, white artificial rabbit began its run around the track. My recollection is that the starter held a button in his hand that was connected to the dog box by a cord. When the mechanical rabbit was in front of the box at a spot the starter was looking for, he pushed the button which caused the entire front of the box to burst up and expose all the dogs to the rabbit at the same time. When they bolted out in their colorful vests with their front legs extended and their necks stretched out toward their quarry, it was the most exciting thing I had ever seen. They raced around the track chasing the rabbit which glided along its arm on the inside rail.

I assume that somewhere, someone was controlling the speed of that mechanical rabbit so the dogs were close behind, but they could never quite catch it. After they had crossed the finish line, the rabbit snapped into a box along the rail and the dogs gathered at the box where they could be retrieved by their handlers. The dogs were excited and winded after the chase, but they appeared happy to me as a young boy as they danced around with their tails wagging. Of course, I only saw the end result. I could not know how these majestic dogs came to be there.

According to the ASPCA, racing greyhounds routinely experience terrible injuries during training and when racing. And, while greyhounds may live a dozen or more years, they were usually retired from racing by two to five years of age because they were either deemed unfit to race after an injury or no longer fast enough to be profitable. Today, most of these retired dogs are sent to rescue groups. In the sordid past of this cruel sport, they were quietly euthanized. Today, there are hundreds of rescue organizations around the country that are ready to step in on their behalf—organizations like Second Chance Greyhounds out of Douglasville, Georgia.

Second Chance described itself as "a dedicated group of volunteers working to place former racing greyhounds into adoptive homes." But Second Chance was unique. Their dogs were fostered and trained by inmates in the Georgia prison system. One of the programs was at the Jenkins County Correctional Facility in Millen, Georgia—a program that provided "an opportunity for inmates to give back to the community while alleviating boredom and tension in prison, resulting in a safer environment for both staff and inmates."

The goal of any training and socialization program is to increase retention of greyhounds in their new adoptive homes. Second Chance offered the added benefit of allowing prison residents to experience first-hand the unconditional love of a pet—a novel experience to many inmates. One fascinating aspect of the program was the blog that provided an inmate report on the dog's progress. Diggory's inmate mentor named the dog Hector and here is a selection of his reports on Hector (Diggory).

3/8/2020 - Hi there from Hector the Handsome Hound! Hector's trainer loves this guy already. He is so intelligent, loving and gentle.

3/29 - This week has been a great week for this sweet pooch. Hector is enjoying his time at Second Chance Greyhounds Academy. He loves being able to roam around freely and play with his toys, but nothing compares to the love he has for his bed. Relaxing during retirement couldn't be sweeter for Hector.

5/10 - Well, we've reached the end of the 10-week training program. Hector's inmate trainer says that he truly enjoyed working with this smart boy. You can't help but smile when you're around Hector! His inmate trainer says that he believes Hector is going to make a great addition to his new forever family.

Greyhounds are trained athletes that are bred for speed, endurance, and an even temperament. They are handled a great deal during their early years by dog walkers, trainers, veterinarians, and others, so they love being around people. But, since they are raised in a monoculture of other greyhounds, they may be uncomfortable around cats and other breeds of dog—especially small dogs that might resemble the fluffy, white rabbits they were trained to chase at the track. Part of the adoption profile is a statement of their tolerance of cats and small dogs. According to his profile, Diggory was not tolerant of either. In real life, however, he learned to get along with my son's rambunctious golden retriever, Libby, and seemed to relish the company of a quiet, seven-year-old cocker named Alice.

The literature describes greyhounds as possessing "superior intelligence" while exhibiting "a quiet but surprising independence." I observed those qualities when Diggory first walked into the room and surveyed all who were present. His independence was evident in the story his owner told of the time Diggory caught a bird in flight. Before Will could react, Diggory had eaten the bird in three gulps—feathers and all. It reminded me of our young, quail hunting cockers that must be trained to give up their birds. They, too, would eat the birds given enough time.

    I feel a sense of kinship with greyhounds. We are both tall and lanky while exhibiting "a quiet but surprising independence." But we do differ in at least a couple of ways. I have never been that guy who could walk in and take over a room full of strangers. In fact, I hate walking into a room full of strangers. And as to possessing "superior intelligence," well, nobody has ever accused me of that, either.

12

Therapy Dogs

Published April 16, 2021

All it takes is a touch. I can feel it when I place my hand on Libby, my son's golden retriever. It is a sense of calm and wellbeing that defies rational explanation. I can't say why I feel it or from whence it comes. It is as though I am in therapy. But make no mistake. Libby is no therapy dog. She is a rambunctious one-year-old that still chases her tail on occasion. The real therapy dogs are in courtrooms comforting distraught, abused children or in rehab centers helping patients in their healing process. They are dogs like Rikki, a small, reddish-colored golden retriever.

I met Rikki about a decade ago at the rehabilitation clinic of the Tallahassee Memorial Hospital (TMH). I was visiting my mother after her knee replacement and Rikki was making her rounds, meeting patients, and bringing encouragement to people who were struggling to get their lives back. Rikki's story has been told by Julie Strauss Bettinger in her 2016 book, *Encounters with Rikki*.

Rikki, it was said, could read a person's body language from a young age. She engaged visually with people by making eye contact, and she would bow her head and tentatively reach out to certain people. She even offered herself to a woman with Parkinson's disease in spite of the woman's uncontrollable tremors. By nine months of age, she and her owner, Chuck Mitchell, were enrolled in an animal therapy training program.

Training a therapy dog involves teaching the dog and handler to interact safely and reliably with the elderly, with young children and with the physically impaired. Dogs learn not to be afraid of elevators, medical equipment, and noisy environments. Trained therapy dogs and their owners volunteer in settings such as schools, hospitals, and nursing homes. One of Rikki's first assignments was as a courthouse therapy dog where she worked with a six-year-old girl who had been sexually abused. Since abused children must tell their painful stories in a courtroom in order for the abuser to be convicted, the frightened little girl learned she could tell her story to the dog—a non-threatening listener she had come to trust.

Therapy dogs are distinct from service dogs. Service dogs are trained to perform specific tasks to help a person with a disability. A service dog might guide an owner who is blind or assist someone who has physical limitations. And while therapy dogs are there to be touched and petted, service dogs are not. Service dogs should not be approached without the owner's permission.

Service dogs must remain with their person at all times and are the only animals that have special access privileges in public places such as on airplanes and in restaurants. Therapy dogs, even the dogs who have earned the American Kennel Club "Therapy Dog" title, do not have that same special access, nor do the third classification of support dogs—those that offer emotional support to their owners.

Although all dogs have an emotional connection with their owner, the AKC suggests that to legally be considered an emotional support dog, the pet (which apparently can be almost any type of animal) needs to be prescribed by a licensed mental health professional to a person with a disabling mental illness. I am a dog person myself, but emotional support animals come in all shapes and sizes. Cats and horses are probably a close second to dogs and I have been known to hug my mules when I am brushing them down before a day of pulling the wagon. Before she retired, my sister-in-law, Sheree Porter, managed the rehabilitation program at TMH. She was a pioneer in their use of therapy dogs like Rikki and she went on to harness the therapeutic powers of birds, horses, and a donkey named Daisey Mae.

But, the days of bringing your emotional support animal on an airplane came to an end in December of 2020 when the federal government enacted a new rule restricting the types of service animals allowed on commercial airline flights. Now, airlines only allow dogs that meet specific training criteria. The new Department of Transportation rule, according to a report on National Public Radio, was in response to a growing backlash in recent years to airline passengers trying to bring all kinds of wild and outlandish animals onto airplanes, including the woman who tried to bring an "emotional support" peacock on board a United Airlines flight in 2018, and the "comfort" turkey that was actually allowed to fly on Delta Airlines back in 2016.

Studies show that interaction with a dog can lower a person's heart rate and cause blood pressure to go down. Petting Libby, I have come to learn, stimulates my production of oxytocin—a hormone that is associated with empathy, trust, and relationship-building. It also releases endorphins which are chemicals produced by the body to relieve stress and pain.

The nature of the dog-human bond is exceptional. It is similar to the classic "pair bond" which is usually between two mated individuals—like my wife and me. She and I enjoy hanging out together. We obey each other (for the most part), we care for each other when necessary, and we greet each other enthusiastically when we reunite. Touch is how we like to connect. We share an innate drive for contact, with a bond that's both pleasurable and hormonal. I hope my wife doesn't find out that all of this could also describe my relationship with my dog.

13

The Dogs of War

Published May 29, 2021

When it comes to books, movies, and TV shows, I am drawn to action and adventure. So, when CBS came out with the new war-drama *SEAL Team* a few years ago, I watched the first few episodes and was hooked. I liked how the Navy SEALs were inserted into a hot zone by helicopter, watercraft, or parachute and how they entered a building in close formation in a carefully choreographed series of moves. But it wasn't the big burly men dressed in camo, wearing night vision goggles, and carrying H&K 416 carbines that drew me in. I was attracted to one particular member of the team—a member whose gear was specially made to fit his unique form and who was often the first one into danger. He was a Belgian Malinois named Cerberus—a war dog.

We humans have been using dogs in battle for centuries. The ancient Greeks and Romans took dogs into battle. The Spanish conquistadors used mastiffs and other large breeds to intimidate native peoples during their exploration of the Americas. And in World War I, the Germans used herding dogs they called *Alsatians* as sentries, messengers, and ammunition carriers. The most famous of these early war dogs, and one I grew up watching on TV, was Rin Tin Tin.

The real Rin Tin Tin was a German shepherd that was rescued from a World War I battlefield by an American soldier and trained for work in silent films. His legacy continued into the 1950s with a television series,

The Adventures of Rin Tin Tin. The magic of television transposed his "war dog" exploits back to the American West of the 1800s.

In WWII, the Marines adopted the Doberman pinscher to help them take back the Pacific Islands from the Japanese. My generation served in the jungles of Vietnam, where thousands of dogs—mostly German shepherds—served alongside our troops. Their handlers affectionately called them "fur missiles."

Today, a new breed of canine soldier has emerged, the Belgian Malinois. This is another herding dog similar to, but smaller than, the German shepherd. Malinois, like German shepherds, have long worked with police departments. In fact, the American Kennel Club noted in the 1908 issue of their newsletter, that five "Belgian Sheepdogs" had been added to the New York City police department.

The Belgian Malinois (or Mal) is one of the top breeds chosen by police departments around the country and they are important members of the U.S. military—where they are officially known as Military Working Dogs. Most of the dogs that work with the elite Navy SEALs are Mals. SEAL dogs, like the TV star Cerberus, are given their own special body armor and are even fitted with night-vision goggles. One of the reasons Belgian Malinois are favored over German shepherds for many military operations is that Mals are lighter, so it's easier for military parachutists to do tandem jumps with their dogs strapped to them. Mals can even be trained to jump on their own, which is reportedly safer for the dogs when they land in water.

I know TV does not represent reality. If a building blows up around you, you probably won't survive. The results of DNA tests don't come back in minutes. And people don't always live happily ever after. But I grew up watching television working dogs like Lassie and Rin Tin Tin perform amazing and dangerous tasks to help their human partners. So, the use of dogs in wartime, seems no worse to me than sending troops—especially those that did not volunteer—into battle. The dogs just need to be treated as valued partners not expendable objects.

The TV SEAL team dog, Cerberus, is portrayed as an equal member of the team. In one episode, he begins to lose his edge and runs away in a firefight. He appears to be lost. But in a subsequent battle we see shades of Lassie and Rin Tin Tin when he saves one of the SEAL team members. The man discovers that Cerberus has a deep knife wound, so he bandages the dog, puts him on his back, and carries him to safety. Cerberus retires with PTSD and goes home to live with the SEAL team member he saved. I like to think that this Hollywood ending is one that would also play-out in real life.

I have always had a special admiration for warfighters—and not because I lived in a town with a Marine Corps base. When I was in my early teens, my older cousin Roger enlisted in the Marines. When he came home from boot camp, I was in awe of him. He was the biggest, baddest dude I had ever seen. Interestingly, he was stationed in Albany at some point in his career. Soon after I moved to Albany, I heard from his brother Johnny, who was in the Air Force, that he and Roger were both stationed in Albany, Georgia at the same time in the 1970s—Johnny at Turner AFB and Roger at MCLB.

Sadly, although my cousin Roger survived several tours in Vietnam, he later succumbed to the devastating effects of the war's PTSD. Roger is still one of my boyhood heroes—one of thousands of war fighters who have sacrificed so we might live free. I wonder if he ever went into battle with one of those "fur missiles" as part of his combat team. In my imagination, he might have led his squad into a jungle firefight following a German shepherd and his handler.

When I first watched *SEAL Team*, I was surprised to see Cerberus jump out of an airplane. I didn't know whether to feel sorry for him or marvel at his bravery. But as I observed the dynamics of the dog's relationship to the team, I came to understand that, TV dramatization notwithstanding, he was part of the team. He was doing what dogs are bred to do. He was carefully trained, lovingly accepted, and prepared to do his part for the "family." Some dogs are bred and trained to hunt birds, some to sniff out contraband, and others to herd sheep. Dogs like Cerberus are warfighters, and we owe the real warfighters—both human and canine—a debt of gratitude for their service and their sacrifice.

14

Guard Dogs Protect the Property We Claim

Published August 2, 2021

I see them as I walk around my neighborhood, peering at me through fences, barking at me in living room windows, and—in at least one unfortunate case—straining against a chain in someone's backyard. They are guard dogs.

The American Kennel Club recognizes seven dog breed groups, including Sporting dogs, Working dogs, Herding dogs, Hounds, Terriers, Toys, and Non-Sporting dogs. But the AKC does not have a category for guard dogs. All dogs, I suppose, are expected to be guard dogs.

Guard dogs, or watchdogs, probably date to the first co-habitation of humans and wolves. Their original job was to protect humans and their domestic herds from dangerous animals and unrecognized humans. They are seen in ancient Greek mythology and were used extensively by the Romans. A second-century mosaic of a black dog was found in a house in Pompeii, enclosed by the Latin quote *"Cave canem!,"* which means "Beware the dog!". We humans, it seems, have long been protective of our property.

Control of property goes back to the very founding of our country. Two hundred fifty years ago, British colonists in the "new world" decided they wanted to break away from British rule and create their own nation. After our success during the American Revolution, we have, as a nation, been obsessed with freedom, independence, and our right to private property. My wife and I have a piece of property. We own a home for which we have a mortgage. We also pay taxes on that home's carefully defined plot, which is located in a particular neighborhood, in a city and county in the state of Georgia. But is it really ours?

The United States, our homeland, was taken by white settlers from the indigenous people who already lived here, and the state of Georgia is land that was seized by the British Empire in the 1700s to protect its North American colonies from the Spanish empire in Florida. In fact, all the boundaries and borders that we like to claim and defend are artificial. Somebody, or some group, bought them or took them by force, then defined them and sold them to us. Yet, we guard them with our lives. As property owners, we put up signs and fences to keep people out. We install elaborate alarms and cameras that connect to our smart phones to warn us of intruders. And we acquire guns and dogs for when people ignore those warnings.

All these artificial and ever-changing boundaries must be confusing to our dogs. They seem to figure out their own homes and yards, but they can get befuddled at the edges. My wife was attacked and bitten by someone's dog as she ran in the street in front of the dog's house. In fact, we have heard reports of several walkers in our neighborhood being bitten by dogs that ran out into the street after them. I suppose the dogs were protecting their territory, but someone needs to tell them that their authority stops at the curb.

If my wife and I decide to sell our home, it will become someone else's patch and they can guard it as they see fit. We will move to a new property and set about marking and protecting our new territory. This, it seems to me, is what the American Dream is all about. I can live where I want, and I can protect where I live with any means necessary. Maybe we'll get a dog that was bred to be a guardian—a dog like the Doberman Pinscher, the bullmastiff, or the boxer. Many of the best guard dogs, however, are general purpose farm dogs like the German Shepherd. This breed has long been synonymous with "police dog" and should be a good dog to serve me and protect my property. But the two most recent dog bites in my neighborhood have been given by German Shepherds that attacked runners in the street. So, I'll probably just stick with a barking dog to warn me of danger.

My son's golden retriever Libby came to stay with us recently. Ian's Atlanta home was on the market and needed to be free of dog hair for a couple of weeks. Libby has visited us plenty of times but never for an extended stay. For the first day or two she was curious about everything, sniffing around the house and yard, and watching through windows as cars and people passed by our house. But by the end of day two, she was more protective of her new territory. Somehow, she had decided that people walking in the street were a threat, and the cars stopped at the stop sign and idling across the road needed to move on. The dog whose idea of dealing with a stranger was once a wag of the tail and a gentle "woof" on their approach followed by licking them into submission, had become a serious guard dog.

    Libby and I are carrying on that time-honored tradition of protecting our home—a home that could be repossessed by the bank if I don't pay my mortgage, on the property that could be seized by the county if I stop paying my taxes, on the land where Native Americans roamed before European settlers kicked them out to the Oklahoma Territory. But I still claim it as "mine," and I have a fence, a shotgun, and a guard dog to prove it.

15

Herding Dogs Are Intelligent, Hard-Working Canines

Published October 21, 2021

One of the most popular shows on television these days is Kevin Costner's modern-day cowboy saga, *Yellowstone*. I watched the first three seasons and will probably watch season four when it comes out from behind its paywall. But not everyone is a fan. My wife, for example, watched about twenty-minutes of the first episode before she gave up on it with the declaration, "There is not one character on this show that I admire." She was right, of course. But I'll probably keep watching anyway—even though it is not a program that would garner much approval from my Sunday school class.

Another criticism I've heard about the show is that there are no dogs on the Yellowstone Ranch. How can you have a working cattle ranch with cowboys, chuckwagons, and livestock but no dogs—no dog to sit on the porch with patriarch John Dutton as he sips his whiskey in the evening, no dog in the horse barn or cattle paddock? In fact, the only dogs I recall seeing were used by cattle rustlers who were stealing some cattle from the Yellowstone Ranch. The scene only lasted a few minutes, but it made an impression on me because the modern-day rustlers used herding dogs to move the cattle quickly and efficiently into a trailer.

As a zookeeper, early in my career, I often had to herd livestock into pens, crates, and trailers. It is not easy when they don't want to go.

That is why I have such admiration for the almost supernatural ability of herding dogs.

My only experience with a herding dog was with Bexley, our seventy-pound mutt that had herding instincts. When we picked her up from the animal shelter nearly twenty years ago, she was a tiny, black ball of fur. Her lineage was unknown, but the shelter had listed her as a "terrier mix." I don't know what kind of terrier they thought she was, but she grew into a black and white version of Old English Sheepdog—a breed that was developed to help drive cattle and sheep to market. Maybe that's why, as she grew older, Bexley had a tendency to bump the backs of our legs and nip at our heels as we moved about the house and yard.

Herding dogs were carved out of the American Kennel Club's (AKC) Working Group in 1983. They were breeds that share the instinctive ability to control the movement of other animals. Herding dogs, which include shepherds, collies, and cattle dogs, were developed to gather, herd, and protect livestock.

One of the most popular breeds of herding dog is the border collie, a beautiful, medium sized, black and white dog that was originally developed on the border of Scotland and England—hence the name. Dog experts widely agree that border collies are intelligent workaholics. They are capable of learning a remarkable number of words and commands, and they are happiest when they are put to work every day. When seen working at shows and herding trials, most people are astonished by their ability to herd sheep into a small pen, guided only by hand signals and whistles from their owners. Border collies are known for staring intensely at members of the flock to intimidate them—a tactic known as using "the eye."

Another sheep herding dog is the Australian Shepherd, or Aussie, a medium-sized worker that also has a keen, penetrating gaze. According to the United States Australian Shepherd Association, there are many theories as to the origin of the Australian Shepherd but, despite its name, the breed as we know it today was developed in the United States. The Australian Shepherd was given its name because of their association with the Basque sheepherders who came to the United States from Australia in the 1800s. The Aussie rose rapidly in popularity with the boom of western riding after World War II, becoming known to the public through appearances in rodeos, horse shows, movies, and television.

Their inherent versatility and trainability made them useful on farms and ranches where American stockmen continued the development of the breed, maintaining their keen intelligence, strong herding instinct and eye-catching appearance.

The Australian Cattle Dog (ACD), also called blue heeler or Queensland Heeler, contains the bloodlines of a variety of other breeds including collies, kelpies, Dalmatians, and even Australia's famous wild dog, the Dingo. The result is a strong compact, symmetrically built working dog that conveys great agility, strength, and endurance. As the name implies, the dog's prime function, and one for which it has no peer, is the control and movement of cattle. The breed is said to be "wary of strangers" which, according to one blogger, means that the odds are your heeler has already met everyone it wants to know. After that they may chase off strangers—even ones who are your new friends.

The use of dogs for herding even extends to the high-Arctic. I recently watched a program about reindeer on the PBS show *Europe's New Wild*. Modern reindeer herders use technology such as GPS systems and snow machines but they also, it appears, use a dog called the Lapponian Herder—a breed that was developed in Finland specifically to herd reindeer.

According to the AKC, the herding instinct in these breeds is so strong that they have been known to gently herd their owners, especially the children of the family. They are alert, courageous, and trustworthy with an implicit devotion to duty. But to be sane, they need to run for hours and use their considerable intelligence to outwit troublesome sheep, not sit inside a house all day while their owner is at work. In her 2002 book *The Other End of the Leash*, dog behavior expert Patricia McConnell bemoans the public's interest in having working and herding dogs as pets. Border collies, for example, may be an ideal size and have beautiful coloring, but McConnell suggests that they are "as ill-suited to most households as mountain goats." Experts recommend that herding dog owners participate with their dog in some sort of work, sport, or regular exercise to keep them mentally and physically fit.

Although our dog Bexley somehow had these herding instincts hard-wired into her makeup, she had little else in common with these pure-bred herding dogs. Bexley died a few years ago, but I don't recall her being a particularly agile or versatile workaholic. If she had a penetrating gaze, it was well hidden by the mop of black fur that covered her eyes between haircuts. And she definitely missed out on the intelligence genes. In fact, the folks who ran the kennel where we regularly boarded her dubbed Bexley a "clown in a dog suit." As lovable as she was, Bexley wasn't going to outsmart anybody—even a herd of sheep

16

A Time to Stop and Smell the Flowers

Published April 2, 2020

    I always imagined the quote about stopping and smelling the roses had come from some famous poet—perhaps Tennyson, Byron, or even Shakespeare. But I was wrong. It was golfer Walter Hagen who said it in his 1956 book *The Walter Hagen Story*. But to be clear, he didn't mention roses. The quote is: "You're only here for a short visit. Don't hurry. Don't worry. And be sure to smell the flowers along the way."

    It was good advice. Smelling the flowers is one of life's great joys and being married to a gardener has been a massive pleasure for me during these days of self-isolation. My wife spends an enormous amount of time in her garden. My job is to keep the grass mowed, tote the odd bale of pine straw, and stay out of the way. Karen does the rest.

    Much of the garden I am enjoying during these difficult days came out of another difficult time. When Hurricane Michael roared through South Georgia in October 2018, our neighborhood was hit hard. We had a pine tree fall on our house, as did our neighbors on both sides. The tree broke off about eight feet from the ground, which allowed it to hinge down like a meat-cleaver and slice our garage roof from wall to wall. You know it is bad when people stop their cars and get out to take a picture. It took nearly a year of construction, but the house has been restored.

The tree damage in the back yard was a different story. Two massive pine trees were uprooted, and one fell across our in-ground swimming pool, smashing the ladder, diving board, and a section of the concrete pool deck. A huge crane had to be called in to lift the tree off the pool. We spent weeks pulling branches and pine needles out of the water, only to discover the pool was leaking from somewhere. Very little of the damage was covered by insurance. It would cost more to repair than to remove. So, we made the painful decision to take the pool out.

Selfishly not wanting to increase the amount of lawn I would need to mow, I suggested to my wife that we replace the pool with a formal garden. She went for it.

Once the pool was filled in, we staked out a perfect rectangle in its place and installed planted areas where the pool deck once was. In place of water, we had a couple of smaller planters, and a bed of gravel with steppingstones. In the middle of the garden—an homage to the pool that once occupied the space—we placed a large, blue urn with water bubbling down its side into a basin. Three ceramic goldfish bobbed in its bowl.

One of the things I have come to appreciate is that a garden, to a true gardener, is much more than just a collection of plants. It is filled with old friends. It contains memories. It tells a story.

The pass-along plants, for example, came from somewhere or someone. We have a rose bush she calls Mrs. Meyers' Rose. She got a start of it from her mother's yard in Louisville, but her mother's bush came from her grandmother's house. And grandma got it from someone named, you guessed it, Mrs. Meyers. She has another rose that we transplanted from a rental property we once owned—a rescue rose. Friends gave her the purple coneflowers and the white iris. Her yellow flag iris came from the Albany Garden Club's plant exchange.

She nurtures her garden and protects her plants when necessary. Her Grancy Greybeard tree is currently covered in white, feathery flowers. But since it grows next to the garage that had to be rebuilt after the hurricane, she placed a fence around it and put the workmen on notice.

And when the deer in our neighborhood decided that the lilies and hydrangeas in the front yard were good eating, she began spreading animal repellant granules by the gallon and had me build wire cages over the hydrangeas.

Karen is not much into growing vegetables, but we are well stocked with basil for her pesto sauce and mint for the mint juleps we serve at our Kentucky Derby party. She has small Meyer lemon and satsuma orange trees, and she is proud of her huge loquat tree. She grew it from a seed I brought home from a tree in Chehaw Park. It is now covered with fruit—and squirrels.

For years, we have drawn pleasure from our garden. We never imagined that one day we would be confined to our yard and that simple enjoyment would become a refuge. I realize that not everyone is as fortunate as I am, but as I walk the neighborhood, I see evidence that everyone can enjoy. Azaleas, dogwoods, and other flowers are blooming everywhere.

We are trying to be good citizens by remaining isolated and avoiding contamination. We don't do it out of an obsessive fear, but rather a sense of community. I don't want some doctor or nurse having to worry about me being critically ill when all I had to do was stay home and smell the flowers.

A wind chime hangs from our screen porch, tapping out its dissonant, luminous melody. It lifts my spirits and complements the sound of the birds, squirrels, and carpenter bees that surround me. The flowers and wind chimes help me appreciate the beauty of nature and, in these dark days, I'll take all the help I can get.

17

Creating New Rituals in the Time of the Coronavirus Pandemic

Published April 9, 2020

I am looking forward to Easter this year. Sunday, April 12th, 2020, is one of the most important days on this year's Christian calendar and I will be there—at least in spirit. For my entire life, the Easter routine has been to get dressed up and go to church. That routine will not change this year, even in a time of social distancing. Well, the get dressed up part will change because I won't be in church physically. The rituals that I enjoy inside my church will change because I can't actually be there. But I am practicing *physical* distancing, not *social* distancing, so I can participate in my church service online and have some serious social closeness. On Sunday morning at 10:30, I will turn on my television, listen to the music, participate in the prayers, and hear a message of encouragement from my pastor. A sidebar on our media feed will tell me who else is participating. We have over two hundred people on a typical Sunday. I wonder how many we will "see" on Easter as I keep my routine of attending church, but not the ritual of a normal service.

During this time of enforced isolation, I have come to appreciate that I have two support patterns that help to structure my life—routine and ritual—and they are not the same. My routines are those habits that give form to my day. I eat breakfast, brush my teeth, and go for a walk. My routines have become more important as I have gotten older. I organize my days well in advance in a notebook I keep by my chair. My wife keeps her list of things to do in the kitchen.

A ritual is different. It is more ceremonial and often connected to an organization. When we participate in a ritual, like going to a place of worship on a particular day, we make a commitment to join other people in a rite of passage. Whether it is a wedding, a birthday celebration, or a graduation, all demand particular behaviors and even socially acceptable clothing. Easter, for example, is typically a time for extravagant attire—our Sunday best.

Rituals can be ancient and mysterious. They can even be considered sinister. We Freemasons have been practicing our rituals for hundreds of years. I always found great comfort when the lodge door was closed, and the Tyler was seated outside, even when the only purpose of the meeting was to practice our rituals. But that secrecy surrounding Masonic rituals has also given rise to conspiracy theories—even though Masonic fraternities contribute millions of dollars every year and support such open and appreciated charities as the free hospitals of the Scottish Rite and the Shriners.

We can't control rituals or change them. They are usually set for us. That is what makes them rituals. They connect us to an organization, to our community, and sometimes to society in general. Rituals are what we have lost for the time being. But we can still have routines to reinforce a sense of control over our everyday lives.

Before I went into my self-imposed isolation, my life was ruled by routine. I was up at 5:30 every morning to read the newspaper and write. I walked in the mornings, went to the gym at 2:00, and ate dinner at 6:00 in front of the local news. Monday through Saturday, I alternated between a three-mile walk and a trip to the gym. I did yoga exercises twice a day and looked forward to my wife coming home from work at around 4:00. Sundays were set aside for church, followed by lunch at a restaurant.

Now, most of that is out the window. My routines have changed. I still take my morning walks and do yoga exercises in the bedroom, but my wife no longer comes home at 4:00—because she is already here. My gym is closed, as is my church and all the restaurants we once visited for Sunday lunch. Once a week, we venture out to the grocery store or drug store, careful to utilize the face masks she made for us. But otherwise, my days, like the days of most everyone else, are filled with… well, monotony.

My isolation shelters me from the world's troubles but, somehow, I sense the anguish of job loss and illness. I recently experienced the death of a close friend. There is no way to sugar coat what is going on. But I see hope in these sad times. I see families riding bikes together, I see couples walking dogs, I see children playing croquet on the front lawn. People are sitting on porches and patios just talking. During one morning walk, I noticed two neighbor ladies walking together. They were far in the distance, heading my way, and something struck me as odd. It took me a while to figure out what it was. One lady was walking along the curb while the other was in the middle of the street—about six feet away. They were not in the same family unit and were honoring each other's social distance.

On that same walk, I saw another unusual sight. A woman was running toward me pushing a stroller—one of those big, three-wheeled jogging strollers. As I caught her eye to nod hello, something was a little off. She was in good shape, but a seemed little old to be pushing babies around in a stroller. I glanced into the stroller, expecting to see a grandchild. Imagine my surprise at having my gaze met by a dog. It was a big dog—maybe a yellow lab—and he looked pretty content lying there bouncing along in a baby carriage. He was a little gray around the muzzle and looked to be at the age when running alongside his companion might have been difficult, but she had figured out a way to include him, anyway.

When necessary, we invent new routines to give us comfort and some sense of control. And we even give a nod to some of our rituals. Our church, for example, has asked us to post a photo or a brief video of what we will be wearing to church on Easter Sunday. Not the all-dressed-up, Sunday-best outfits we would wear if we were going to the church building. We are to show what we will be wearing as we watch from our homes. For me, it has been an old t-shirt, some shorts, and my comfy bedroom slippers. For this Easter, I might shave and put on a clean t-shirt.

At the end of one of our first days in isolation, I suggested to my wife that we take a walk every evening after dinner. She not only agreed, but she also decided to document the walk by posting a photo on social media of our feet in a different pose each night and one photo of something interesting or beautiful that we had seen. She has done this every night. It is now a touchstone of our time together. A new ritual that keeps us sane in these insane times.

18

Wrens in the Driveway

Published April 19, 2020

What is it about wrens? While most birds are content to nest in the trees and shrubs around my house, the wrens seem to want to nest *inside* my house—or, at least, in my garage. The minute I open my garage door in the morning, they begin to flit in and out looking for that perfect spot among the boxes, bins, and baskets. My garage door stands open most of the day since my wife and I are both retired. The wrens are our only outside visitors, and they keep pretty busy.

When we removed a pile of leaves and sticks from an old dishpan on a shelf in the garage, we immediately suspected the wrens because they were still flying in and out of the garage every time we opened the door. In the wild, wrens are known to pile twigs, pine straw, and leaves into the cavities they choose. This provides a platform on which to build a nest. The cup itself is built into a depression in the twigs and lined with soft materials like feathers, grasses, and animal hair. Once the nest is complete, the female will lay from three to ten white or gray eggs which they will incubate for up to two weeks.

A couple of days after we removed the debris that might have become a nest, I observed them carrying pine straw and leaves into an old coat rack next to the garage door. The coat rack held several extension cords that were coiled on its hooks and apparently made a great platform for a nest. What's better, two of my yard hats—an expensive Tilley hat topped by an old bucket hat—provided a roof. It took two days of steady work for them to build a fine-looking nest. I was willing to give up the use of my extension cords and hats, but a bigger problem was apparent. The nest was inside my garage, and I wasn't willing to leave it open for the duration. So, I moved the coat rack a few feet and set it outside the garage. That's the last I saw of the wrens.

My wife and I have long been bird watchers. We enjoy observing them, identifying them, and attracting them to our backyard. We also enjoy the exotic birds when we travel. Our bookshelves at home include volumes on the birds of Britain and Europe, Belize, Costa Rica, Canada, and East Africa. My wife is an artist and, after our trip to Belize a few years ago, she documented our experience by doing a large painting that hangs in our bedroom. It represents a lush, tropical landscape with a Mayan ruin in the distance. But the painting features birds—collared aracari, blue-crowned motmot, violaceous trogon, great kiskadee, and ferruginous pigmy owl.

During my own travels, I have searched for the elusive resplendent quetzal in the cloud forests of Costa Rica, marveled at the primitive hoatzin on a tributary of the Amazon River, and gingerly stepped over nesting blue-footed boobies in the Galapagos Islands. But I receive at least as much pleasure observing the birds in my southwest Georgia yard. One day, I had to stop working in the backyard to watch a pair of Rufous-sided towhees scratching around in the leaf-litter. Later, I peered out my front door at the bluebirds catching insects on the front lawn.

One afternoon, my wife called me to the back porch to see a flock of a dozen or so cedar waxwings that had piled one on top of one another into our concrete birdbath. That birdbath is frequently used by mockingbirds, mourning doves, and others. It is also the source of bird fights. We recently watched a female cardinal chase two blue jays out of it and then saw a tiny bluebird chase away that female cardinal.

One evening, we were eating dinner on the back porch and, as the evening sun was setting behind me, I saw a distinctive shadow flitting across the brick wall of the house. It was our first ruby-throated hummingbird of the season. He was looking for the feeder that hung there last year. How in the world did he find that spot outside my kitchen window from wherever he had spent the winter? That evening, I prepared the simple syrup we keep in the feeder all summer and we have enjoyed the hummers ever since.

And our bird watching continues into the night with the serenade of barred owls hooting back and forth sounding like they are asking, "Who cooks for you?"

It took me a lifetime of travel to appreciate the fact that the birds that fly in and out of my backyard are as wild and exotic as any I have seen around the world. Birds represent the freedom we all yearn for, and they inspire in me an appreciation of nature. And then there are the contrary little wrens.

After seven days of watching the nest, I decided the wrens had abandoned it. But as I approached the coat rack to move it back inside the garage, a wren flew out. She soon came back and sat tight. A male wren delivered bugs to feed her.

Wrens, according to the Cornell University Bird Lab, prefer nest sites in open woodland. They tend to avoid heavily wooded areas where it's hard to see predators coming. They will nest in old woodpecker holes, natural crevices, and nest boxes provided by humans. If they can't find any of those spots, they will improvise. In my case, they liked an old coat rack at the edge of a South Georgia driveway.

My *Peterson Field Guide* describes wrens as "small energetic brown birds; stumpy, with slender, slightly decurved bills; tails often cocked." That cocked, upturned tail looks to me like a one-fingered salute—the sign of a haughty, "I'll nest where I please" personality. I expect they would nest on my living room bookshelf if I left the front door open for them.

19

Celebrating Earth Day at Fifty

Published April 21, 2020

I don't know about you, but the last thing I needed during the global pandemic was more bad news. So, as we celebrated the fiftieth anniversary of Earth Day, I vowed not look at the perils we were in because of climate change. I wanted to find something to celebrate. So I found hope by looking back on my fifty-year career working with animals—hope that maybe things were not as grim as they appeared to be.

A few years ago, I wrote a little book called *The View from a Wagon: Five Lessons for Living Life in the Slow Lane*. It was intended to be positive and hopeful. During the pandemic, with plenty of time on my hands, I wrote a follow-up book titled *Lessons from the Zoo: Ten Animals that Changed My Life*.

In it, I explain how I learned to trust from working around elephants and how not to be too trusting after dangerous encounters with big cats. I reflected on the animals that taught me to face my fears (reptiles), to appreciate life (dogs), and to apply the golden rule in everything I do (apes). I have learned from the animals, and I have witnessed dramatic and positive changes in the way we interact with them.

When I was a young zookeeper at Busch Gardens nearly fifty years ago, the black rhinos frightened me. They were flighty, unpredictable, and always took an aggressive approach to any situation. It was charge first and ask questions later—three-thousand pounds of meanness and aggression. Any veterinary procedures required a tranquilizer dart, and it seemed to me that even then, things never seemed to go well.

When we received two black rhinos at Chehaw Wild Animal Park in 2006, I expected we might be in for some rough times. Dubya and Sam Houston were a couple of adult males that came from a breeding ranch in Texas and were semiwild. The first time we locked one of them in our squeeze chute, he went crazy, banging the bars so hard we thought he would either kill himself or break out of the cage and kill us.

But animal care professionals had learned much about animal behavior in the previous few decades. When I was deputy director at the Toledo Zoo in the 1990s, for example, we brought in trainers to help us work with the animals in our collection. These were the people who had learned to train killer whales and parrots. They were confident that their use of something called operant conditioning—using food rewards to elicit a behavior—would work with other species. They were spectacularly successful, and the animal business was transformed. The keepers at Chehaw decided to try operant conditioning on our new rhinos.

After several tedious months of convincing the rhinos that we meant them no harm, they learned to do just about anything for a piece of sweet potato. They would place their noses on the outstretched hand of a keeper when commanded to "target." They stood calmly while staff rubbed them or checked inside their ears. They tolerated groups of rowdy schoolchildren entering their night house. And, most remarkably, I watched a rhino stand still enough to allow a veterinarian to stick a needle into an ankle to draw a blood sample while it calmly took another piece of sweet potato from its keeper.

Thanks to some patience and many hours of training and building trust, these animals went from frightened and insecure, to comfortable and docile. Their quality of life improved immensely as they settled into a life of routine activities punctuated by enough changes to make life interesting. The zoo business has evolved during my career, and it excites me to imagine how it might change in the next forty or fifty years. Come to think of it, the world as we know it is likely to change, too.

Richard Louv, in his book *Our Wild Calling*, interviewed one provocative eco-theologian who suggests that the world is a multi-species community of which humans are just a part. But we humans refuse to join the club. Is it because of some divine spark—our belief in God—that we have chosen to separate ourselves from the rest of God's creation? I wonder if that is what God intended.

We may feel that we are separate and alone as a species—above the fray, as it were—but at the end of the day, COVID-19 proved that we are not so special. What will it take for us to give up our exalted and delusional position as rulers of the earth and recognize that we must become part of the earth in partnership with plants and animals?

If we learned anything from the viral pandemic, it was something we have heard over and over, "We are all in this together." The virus showed that we are not in control, because the natural world—of which viruses are a part—affects all of us equally, whether we are white, black, Latino; Christian, Jew, Muslim; American, Italian, Chinese. Global climate change may not be as dramatic as a virus that had the entire world hiding in our homes, but it does affect all of us just the same.

When Dubya and Sam Houston arrived at Chehaw, they were adult rhinos and, by some measures, too old to learn "new tricks." But the rhinos taught me that we are never too old to learn. I earned a master's degree from the University of Georgia at the age of sixty, I self-published a novel at sixty-three, learned to drive a mule wagon and wrote a book about it at sixty-six, and now, at the age of seventy I am learning a new world order. As the celebrated Spanish author Miguel de Cervantes wrote in the early 1600s in his classic work *Don Quixote*: "It's good to live and learn."

This is a marvelous and complex earth on which we live. I have a feeling we are all going to be learning more about the natural world—and about ourselves—as we begin to venture back into it. On this the fiftieth anniversary of Earth Day, I can't say I am looking forward to what awaits, but the more I learn, the less intimidated I am at the prospect. I think I'll go out and do something good for the earth today. How about you?

20

On the Verge of a Coronavirus Book Crisis

Published April 29, 2020

We had a sheltering-in-place crisis of sorts in my house during the early days of the pandemic. The public library was closed, and my wife almost ran out of books to read. We are both avid readers and like to alternate between fiction and non-fiction, and she was down to one of each. You need to understand; Karen is not just any reader. She is an expert, don't-try-this-at-home reader with a master's degree in library science and a seat on the library board. While I struggle to get through a book a month, she breezes through a book a week, and she usually has two going at once. She is a fan of cozy, British mysteries and was working her way through the entire collection of Agatha Christie books. In non-fiction, she had just finished Walter Isaacson's five-hundred-page biography of Benjamin Franklin.

My first clue that we had a problem came when she dropped the book she was reading—apparently by an author who was new to her—and exclaimed in disgust, "This reads like a James Bond movie. I'm twenty-five pages in, and this guy has already slept with two women and had a car chase."

Definitely not her cup of tea! Where was Hercule Poirot when she needed him?

I had been reading a lot, too. I also like British mysteries, but I favor the action thrillers more. I had just read author Lee Childs' latest Jack Reacher novel, *Blue Moon*. When I alternate between fiction and non-fiction, I will read something by David Baldacci, Michael Connelly, or John Grisham then throw in the latest Richard Louv book or anything by Annie Dillard. At the time, I was reading Erik Larson's, *The Splendid and the Vile: A Saga of Churchill, Family, and Defiance During the Blitz*.

I wondered if other people were reading more those days. I saw them out walking and riding bikes, but what went on inside my neighbors' homes, I couldn't say. Perhaps they were working on puzzles to help pass the time. We had a five-hundred-piece hummingbird jigsaw puzzle spread out on our dining room table and a one-thousand-piece Frida Kahlo puzzle still in the box.

A lot of people were absorbed in a Netflix "documentary" called *Tiger King: Murder, Mayhem, and Madness*. I have plenty of murder, mayhem, and madness in my books. In fiction, nobody does murder and mayhem better than Lee Child's character, Jack Reacher. I'm talking about the 6'5", 250 pounds of "bone and muscle" hero, not the 5'7" actor who played him in the movies.

If you want true murder, mayhem, and madness you could try Erik Larson. How can you go wrong with book titles like *The Devil in the White City: Murder, Magic, and Madness at the Fair That Changed America*? Or how about *In the Garden of Beasts: Love, Terror, and an American Family in Hitler's Berlin*?

Books bring me pleasure and they transport me to a different time and place. They provide an escape from reality. But they occasionally surprise me and bring me back to the present. For example, in the book I was reading at the time, author Erik Larson noted the famous speech that Prime Minister, Winston Churchill, gave to the British House of Commons on 20 August 1940. In it, he referred to the heroic stand taken by members of the Royal Air Force (RAF) against the onslaught of the German Luftwaffe during the Battle of Britain.

Never in the field of human conflict was so much owed by so many to so few.

Churchill might as well have been talking about the medical professionals of the day who were taking a heroic stand against our invisible enemy, the coronavirus. Books will be written about those heroes someday.

The book crisis in my house would be over soon because—as I assured my wife—the public library would be opening any day. After all, if the governor had determined that barber shops, tattoo parlors, and bowling alleys were safe and essential, surely we could figure out how to mask up and keep our distance in the library.

I wasn't sure she was buying it, but I sure did hope I was right. I was nearing the end of my own stack of books and starting to eye hers. That five-hundred-page Benjamin Franklin biography loomed large—literally

21

Feeling Squirrely?

Published May 22, 2020

I may be the only person I know who actually likes squirrels. Everybody else either hates them as pests or is indifferent to them. Squirrels have even entered our American vernacular as a somewhat derogatory adjective. Squirrely, according to Merriam-Webster, describes a person who is unusually active, restless, or lacking stability and control. If that is not bad enough, the dictionary goes on to suggest a squirrely person is "morally dubious or questionable."

The eastern gray squirrels that inhabit our neighborhoods are not morally dubious, but they are so ubiquitous we hardly notice them. They seem to be everywhere. Their original home was the oak, hickory, and walnut forests of eastern North America. That is because they eat primarily nuts and they prefer the cover that the dense shade trees provide. In nature, their numbers are controlled by owls, foxes, coyotes, and bobcats. In our neighborhoods, the squirrel population seems to be controlled by cars—and the occasional electrical transformer.

I don't claim to be an expert on squirrels. I have worked with other rodents (guinea pigs, prairie dogs, and capybara) but the only tree squirrel I ever worked with as a zookeeper was a beautiful squirrel from Southeast Asia, the Prevost's squirrel. Its striking, tricolored markings—a white stripe along the side that separates a black back, and a chestnut red belly—helped me appreciate the elegance of squirrels for the first time.

There are nearly two-hundred-fifty species of squirrels in the world. They are indigenous to the Americas, Eurasia, and Africa, and they come in a variety of sizes. The tiniest squirrel is the aptly named African pygmy squirrel. It is only five inches long from nose to tail. Others reach sizes shocking to those who are only familiar with common tree squirrels. The Indian giant squirrel, for example, is three feet long and could chase a small dog. Even in South Georgia, we have a variety of squirrels in sizes ranging from delicate flying squirrels to robust, colorful fox squirrels.

Some squirrels burrow underground and inhabit vast subterranean towns (prairie dogs). Some live on the ground, scurrying around forest floors (chipmunks). And some, like our gray squirrels, are terrific climbers adapted to life in the trees but who also spend time on the ground in search of food such as nuts, acorns, berries, and flowers. Eastern gray squirrels are commonly seen everywhere from woodlands to city parks. They are social and vocal, using tail signals and vocalizations to communicate.

As their large eyes indicate, squirrels have excellent vision, which is especially important for these tree-dwelling species. Many also have a good sense of touch, with vibrissae (stiff hairs that are used as organs of touch) on their limbs as well as their heads. The teeth of squirrels follow the typical rodent pattern, with large incisors (for gnawing) that grow throughout their life, and cheek teeth (for grinding) that are set back behind a wide gap.

Tree squirrels live in a three-dimensional world like big city apartment dwellers. They are equally adept on the ground, climbing up and down trees, and scampering about on branches high in the air. I imagine that they have preferred pathways to get from place to place just like I do. When I go from my house to the grocery store, I have a preferred route down Old Dawson Road and left on Pointe North. The squirrels seem to operate in the same manner. I see them hopping from the big oak tree in my backyard, onto the wooden privacy fence where they walk along its top to a small tree in my neighbor's yard. I wonder where they are going. Do they know there is food ahead? Surely, they are not just wandering aimlessly—out for a walk, as it were.

We recently had to cut down a large loquat tree in our back yard. It had been damaged by Hurricane Michael and we finally grew tired of looking at the broken branches and dead leaves. We did wait for it to

finish bearing fruit for the year as a nod toward the squirrels and birds—
or was it in deference to my wife who would come in from the garden
with both hands full of ripe, delicious fruit. I wonder what the squirrels
thought as they surveyed our cruel action from high in the oak tree. Their
days of romping in its branches and gorging on loquats were over. They
were forced to watch helplessly as their favorite dining spot was wiped
out in a few hours.

Since our last dog died a couple of years ago, the squirrels have had
free rein in our yard. We have had a few problems with them gnawing
the PVC plumbing vents on our roof but otherwise they cause no problems. That may be because the only bird feeder we have is filled with
sugar-water for the hummingbirds. If we had seed feeders, we would
probably be at war with the furry creatures, like most bird lovers I know.

Squirrel-proof bird feeders are their own industry. They come with
names like *squirrel proof*, *squirrel buster*, and *squirrel-be-gone*. Bird
lovers can purchase special poles and baffles to thwart the acrobatic,
seed-loving rodents or they can use whatever is at hand, like grease or a
toy slinky applied to the pole. Then there is something called the rule of
5–7–9. Experts suggest that feeders be placed out of reach of the squirrels who it is said cannot jump more than five feet up from the ground,
won't jump more than seven feet across from a tree or building, and are
reluctant to drop more than nine feet onto a feeder from above. How they
came up with those numbers I am not sure. I wonder if they account for
the Olympic champion long-jumping squirrel who can jump eight feet
across from a branch?

My brother Don is an avid bird enthusiast who lives in South
Carolina. He once kept several bird feeders in his lovely suburban backyard, but his tree-covered property was, of course, ideal squirrel habitat.
The squirrels would clean out his bird feeders in minutes. Don had tried
baffles, greased poles, and expensive squirrel-proof feeders, but nothing
seemed to work.

When I visited him several years ago, he seemed to have hit on a solu-
tion. He had run a wire between two trees and suspended his feeder from
another wire halfway between the trees, far enough that squirrels could
not leap the distance (presumably following the rule of 5–7–9). But as
extra insurance against the squirrels walking the wire, he ran it through a
continuous line of plastic, two-liter soft drink bottles that were fastened

together with duct tape. In order to get to the feeder, a squirrel would need to walk these rolling soda bottles like a lumberjack in a log-rolling contest. I believe he was successful, but he had spent hours on the contraption and its appearance was—let's just say *rustic*.

    I like having squirrels in my yard. We also have rabbits, box turtles, several species of lizards, and a few garter snakes. It is my own little wildlife refuge, and, in these days of isolation, I need all the company I can get. When I stretch out on my porch in the afternoon, I doze to the sound of wind chimes, bird songs, and squirrels chattering in the trees. I wonder if they are warning me that the neighbor's cat is on the prowl again or they are just feeling squirrely.

22

The Art of the Walk

Published June 8, 2020

Being married to an artist sure is eye opening. I mean that literally. I see things differently when she is involved—at least I try to. When she is picking out paint colors for a room, she might come home from the paint store with a handful of those little color samples. If we are looking for a neutral color to paint a room, she may have a dozen different shades of beige from which to choose—and they all look alike to me. But after being married for nearly forty years, I have learned to keep quiet and just nod in agreement when she asks for my opinion.

"Oh, yes," I will agree. "That one has too much blue in it and this one is a little too yellow."

On the evening we began our self-imposed COVID isolation, we got up from the dinner table and decided to go for a walk. For the next few months, we walked about a mile and a half every evening, rain or shine. She decided, before that first walk, to document the experience on social media with two photos—one of something interesting or beautiful (flowers, birds, clouds, etc.) and one photo of our feet. I thought that was about the dumbest idea I had ever heard. Who wants to see a photo looking down at our four feet? Fortunately, I kept my mouth shut.

After dozens of walks, my artistic wife managed to make a daily social media post in which no two feet-photos were alike. Our feet were seen walking and standing. We posed on broken concrete and pebbled asphalt, and on yellow lines and white lines. We stood on sewer manhole covers and water valve covers. As we started our evening stroll and she began to look for two unique photos, I discovered that I enjoyed helping her. It was like those I-spy games we played as kids on long trips. I am amazed at how much beauty and interest surrounds us when we look for it. She was the artist, and I was the apprentice.

Enduring weeks of isolation to avoid an invisible threat made us feel somewhat helpless. So, another benefit of that evening walk was that it gave us some degree of control. We walked no matter what. We talked without distraction—no phones, no internet—unless we saw something of interest to share. We were together all day and all night, but that twenty-minute walk was the highlight of the day. We were truly alone and truly together.

On Sunday, May 31st, her photo of interest was our long shadows cast in the street by the late evening sun. It was a hot, summer sun and our shadows revealed that I was carrying a sweat towel and she had one of those paper fans with a wooden stick handle. Some people call them funeral fans. On this evening, it was keeping the gnats away—a gnat fan. Summer, we noticed, was here and walking seemed more of a chore than a treat. It was time for a change in our coronavirus routine.

The next evening, on Monday, June 1st, her social media post read, "Walk #80 is in the books and is the last one until the temperature falls back to tolerable levels (in South Georgia that may be in October)."

Our friends and relatives around the country responded.

From Kentucky, "I've enjoyed the journey."

From Ohio, "Awesome you were doing that."

From Atlanta, "I'll miss seeing your feet."

Now, as I look back over those eighty days of isolation—punctuated by furtive, masked-up trips to the grocery store—the thing I miss most is getting up from supper, piling the dishes in the sink, and lacing up my walking shoes. I miss the intimate conversation with my wife in the cool evening air. I miss observing the beauty that surrounds us as seen through the eye of an artist. And, as my cousin from Atlanta noted, I miss seeing where our feet would end up. It is a good thing I kept my mouth shut and did not tell my wife what a dumb idea that foot photo was. Our walking feet not only propelled us around the neighborhood. They apparently stepped into a number of lives in the process.

23

Urban Deer: Walking the Fine Line between Natural Beauty and Pest

Published October 1, 2020

When I was growing up, big boys weren't supposed to cry at the movies. I knew that. But when I was nine or ten years old, two movies did make me cry and probably helped shape the rest of my life. The worst one, the movie that broke my heart, was *Old Yeller*. When Old Yeller, the family dog, had to be put down because he had been bitten while protecting his family from a rabid wolf, I cried like a baby. I wonder if that had something to do with my lifelong love affair with dogs.

  The second movie that touched my heart and made me cry was Bambi. Even though it was only a cartoon, I couldn't understand why someone would shoot Bambi's mother. This may be one of the reasons I have always had a soft spot for deer. I have worked with all types of deer—reindeer, red deer, and roe deer; elk, moose, and muntjac; fallow deer, barasingha, and Pere David's—but white-tailed deer are my favorite. When I was a senior keeper at the Toronto Zoo, I had a hand raised white-tail named Patricia that followed me around like a pet dog when I cleaned her pen. She was wild enough to breed and raise babies, but she was also imprinted on humans. Imprinting is cute when the deer is a female. But I once worked with an imprinted male that saw me as a rival during his rut. I stopped going in with him when he charged at me with his head lowered and I had to hold on to his antlers and back my way to the gate.

The range of the white-tailed deer is huge, from the Arctic Circle in Canada to parts of South America. If you look up the diet of white-tailed deer, you will see leaves, twigs, fruits, and nuts, as well as lichens and fungi listed. Place a group of deer in a heavily wooded area, fence them in, and they will eat everything from the ground up to about six feet. The entire area will look like someone when through with a chainsaw and manicured all the vegetation to a precise height—a height that is known in wildlife management as the "browse-line." But white-tailed deer will readily turn to cultivated vegetation when available in urban areas—like my neighborhood. You might even list the daylilies in my wife's garden as a favorite food.

Last summer, for the first time in fifteen years, our deer problem escalated. We looked out the kitchen window into our fenced backyard one morning to see a doe and fawn standing on the lawn. When we went out to chase them off, mama easily jumped the fence to escape while the baby walked through the slats. That afternoon, Karen was out extending the height of our fence by stringing twine from tree to tree and fastening strips of tinfoil. Problem solved—for now.

Deer are abundant in our land-locked urban neighborhood. I see them on my early morning walks and late in the evenings when driving home from some appointment. They are probably safer in my neighborhood than they are in the woods. I wonder if they know that. Do they pass the word to each other that the eating is good, and no one is shooting?

People have been hunting deer for thousands of years. Deer, along with gazelles, are designated in the book of Deuteronomy as "clean" animals that are given by God for humans to eat. And in Georgia, we take that God-given right seriously. Georgia's deer hunting season usually opens for archery in mid-September and firearms in mid-October. Out of the more than a million deer that live in Georgia, about a quarter of them are harvested every year. Another fifty thousand are killed on our roadways. But the population remains relatively constant because a female deer will give birth to one or two fawns every year.

It seems ironic that in the fall, when thousands of hunters are getting up before dawn hoping to see a deer, my wife will be trying her best to shoo them away. Since we have successfully kept them out of our backyard, they have adapted to front-yard dining. The daylilies along the road seem to be attracting them. I have not witnessed this, but judging by the grazing pattern, they must be strolling along the road late at night and pausing to eat at the curb without stepping foot on the grass. Then, unfortunately, they see what is up in the yard.

They don't eat our spirea, azaleas, or lantana. They seem to prefer grassy plants like daylilies, agapanthus, and liriope. But hydrangeas are a delicacy. Last year, Karen planted three oak-leaf hydrangeas in the front bed. They were beautiful with large, dark green leaves and delicate, white blossoms. Had we done a little more research, we would have seen this notation on one website: *Deer love to eat this plant.* The hydrangeas never stood a chance. We tried erecting chicken wire cages over them, but we eventually transplanted them to the relative safety of the backyard.

Sometimes, when I wake up at night, I will creep to the front window and gaze into the front yard. A few weeks ago, I saw a doe and two fawns standing on the lawn. I was mesmerized by the three deer bathed in the soft glow of moonlight and I was reminded of Patricia, my long-ago "pet" deer. The spell was broken when I realized they were standing in the daylilies. I remembered Bambi and knew I needed to warn them off. I opened the front door. That was all it took.

Later that summer, Karen upped her game. The deer wouldn't leave those front-yard daylilies alone, and she was at the breaking point. We replaced the hydrangeas with spirea. She spent one evening cutting a disposable, aluminum roasting pan into little squares and strung the bits of shiny metal with twine in the front yard flower beds as a deterrent. She purchased three-pound containers of animal repellent granules to spread around the edges of the beds. It claimed to ward off everything from deer to shrews. I never saw a shrew in my yard, so at least it works on them.

We pride ourselves on having a wildlife-friendly yard. We feed the hummingbirds. We have a pond with goldfish and frogs. And we provide space for a pair of box turtles to raise their young. We even welcome any non-venomous snakes that want to hang out in the iris beds. Karen loves wildlife as much as I do but I am worried that one morning, when I walk out in the pre-dawn darkness to get the newspaper, I will find her crouched high above the front yard in my son's tree-stand, wearing his camo gear, and resting our shotgun across her knees. Bambi and her mother had better watch out.

24

Box Turtles 'Fred', 'Wilma' Represent the Quiet Life

Published October 14, 2020

I felt like they should have names, so I called them Fred and Wilma. They had lived in my yard for years. I never knew exactly where their home was, but they appeared once or twice a year like ghosts out of the fog—or I should say out of the iris beds. Sometimes just Fred, sometimes just Wilma, and occasionally one of their offspring. Once, my wife saw Fred and Wilma together right there in the middle of the lawn. That's how we discovered which one was Fred and which one was Wilma. Fred's plastron (bottom of the shell) was concave, allowing him to mount Wilma for breeding. They were box turtles.

The box turtle is a medium-sized, terrestrial turtle, about five to six inches long with a high, rounded shell that is dark with yellow and orange splotches. The front third of the plastron is hinged, allowing the box turtle to close itself inside (hence, the name).

Box turtles are omnivorous and eat everything from mushrooms, fruits, and vegetation to worms, slugs, and insects. These animals are long-lived (perhaps reaching fifty years of age or more) and take over five years to reach maturity. Eastern box turtles mate from around April to October, then hibernate through the colder months from October or November until April.

Common throughout the eastern United States, box turtles are found in a variety of habitats like open hardwood forests and fields or wetland edges. They also did quite well in my backyard. They are survivors that can apparently adapt to an unconventional habitat, unlike their cousin the gopher tortoise.

The gopher tortoise was designated Georgia's state reptile in 1989 and is now listed as "threatened." It is considered a keystone species in the rapidly disappearing longleaf pine/wiregrass ecosystem because its burrows provide shelter for hundreds of other species living in their habitat.

A keystone is the wedge-shaped stone at the apex of a masonry arch. It is the last piece placed during construction and locks all the stones into position, allowing the arch or vault to bear weight. A keystone species is a species on which other species in an ecosystem largely depend. It can be any organism, from animals and plants to bacteria and fungi. It is not necessarily the largest or most plentiful species in an ecological community, but if a keystone is removed, it sets off a chain of events that turns the structure and biodiversity of its habitat into something different.

A keystone might be a predator, like the timber wolf of western North America, which keeps the population and range of their prey in check. Remove a keystone predator, and the population of creatures it once hunted can explode, pushing out other organisms and reducing species diversity.

Keystone prey, which include animals ranging from Antarctic krill to Canadian snowshoe hares, also have a big role to play in the ecosystem. They serve as a critical food source for predator populations. But keystone prey must be resilient creatures, unlike some other types of prey species that are more susceptible to becoming rare or extinct within an ecosystem.

A keystone can also be an ecosystem engineer. Instead of impacting the food supply, animals like beavers, African elephants, and gopher tortoises can create, modify, or maintain the surrounding landscape. They influence the prevalence and activities of other organisms and help define the overall biodiversity of their habitat.

So, gopher tortoises are the "influencers" of the animal kingdom. Human influencers are people who use their fame to influence the decisions of the masses. They are mostly people I have never heard of and who are famous for being famous. The only ones I can think of are the Kardashians.

My box turtles, Fred and Wilma, on the other hand, were not influencers or ecosystem engineers. They were like me, just going about their daily lives and quietly minding their own business. I never knew where they were most of the time. I didn't know where they lived, whether they had bred, or where Wilma might lay her eggs. But I was glad they were poking about in the underbrush outside my house, eating mushrooms, worms, and bugs.

Their quiet life represents all of us who lead quiet lives. We can't all be bigshot influencers or keystones, holding our communities together. Some of us just are. We lead lives, as Henry David Thoreau suggested, "of quiet desperation." Most of us are like Fred and Wilma, enjoying life's pleasures, enduring life's pain, and hoping to find a worm or two in the leaflitter of our existence.

25

Lizards in our Midst

Published November 9, 2020

Now that the blazing hot South Georgia weather has broken and I can once again sit outside on my porch, I have become reacquainted with some old friends. I grew up in Florida calling them chameleons, but they are actually green anoles. These five- to eight-inch lizards may be either green or brown depending on environmental conditions. I have always admired the pinkish throat fan that male anoles display in territorial rivalries or when approaching a potential mate. They are common throughout Georgia and can be found almost anywhere perched on trees, fences, and rooftops from suburban woodlands to urban neighborhoods.

Anoles are active by day in warm weather, sunning themselves on vegetation and occasionally charging away from a basking spot to grab an insect or chase off a rival. During cool weather anoles are often found hiding under tree bark, shingles, or in rotten logs. They eat a wide variety of insects, spiders, and other invertebrates. Their ability to change color from bright green to dark brown has given them the nickname chameleon, but their color changing abilities are not nearly as sophisticated as the technicolor changes of true, old-world chameleons.

For the longest time, when I thought of lizards, I thought of the green anole. But as I have grown older, I have come to appreciate and enjoy the diversity of lizards in my yard—lizards like the five-lined skink. Although the same size, skinks and anoles are not easily confused.

Skinks are gray, brown, or black, in background color with five white or yellowish stripes (two on each side and one down the center of the back). Young have a bright blue tail while adult males often develop reddish or orange coloration on the head. Skinks don't have the anole's distinctive pinkish throat fan.

Like the anoles, five-lined skinks also range throughout Georgia, living in almost any habitat, and eating a wide variety of insects, spiders, and other invertebrates. They are reported to be equally at home on the ground and in trees, but in my yard, I mainly see skinks scurrying across the ground.

I have worked with plenty of exotic lizards in my career, including iguanas, tegus, and monitors. They come in all shapes, sizes, and colors. So, when I saw a lizard that was nearly a foot long basking on the ground outside the door to my garden shed, I thought it must be an exotic. I had never seen anything like it, with its enlarged orange head and powerful jaws. I had a hard time getting a good look at it since it scurried under the shed whenever I approached. It was, I came to learn, not an exotic animal. It was a broadhead skink—the largest skink in the southeast, and the largest of the lizards in our region. Female and immature broadheads are similar in appearance to five-lined skinks, but adult male broadhead skinks are unmistakable.

The big male broadhead finally stopped sitting outside my shed. I presume he got tired of my intruding on his habitat and retreated to live in the trees. Although they may be found both on the ground and in trees, broadhead skinks, particularly large males, are more arboreal (tree-dwelling) than any of the other southeastern skinks. When pursued, broadhead skinks generally run for the nearest tree or log and can be quite difficult to capture. Like many other lizards, broadhead skinks will break off their tails when restrained, distracting the predator, and allowing the lizard to escape.

One lizard that had me stumped, however, was the small, four- to five-inch lizard that I saw scurrying away from my grill when I removed the cover. I managed to get a better look one night when I saw it clinging to the outside of my kitchen window. It was unlike any native lizard, with its sticky toe pads, vertical pupils, and large eyes that lack eyelids. It was a Mediterranean gecko—an introduced species.

As its name implies, the Mediterranean gecko is what is known as an old-world lizard. It is common in southern Europe and northern Africa but has been introduced in many tropical areas worldwide, including urban areas in the southeastern United States. In almost all areas, this species is associated with human development, and it is seldom found far from buildings with outdoor lights. They are almost completely nocturnal and are generally light gray or almost white but may have some darker mottling. Their sticky toe pads allow them to climb walls and they are often observed perched on walls and windows around outside lights, waiting to grab insects attracted to the light. By day, these lizards hide in cracks, crevices, and under tree bark—or grill covers.

I appreciated the diversity of lizards in my backyard. Anoles scurried around on the ledges and furniture of my porch while the skinks seemed to prefer the underbrush of the garden leaf-litter. The giant broadhead skink lurked under the shed while the tiny Mediterranean gecko boldly clung to my kitchen window. They all seemed to get along, occupying their own little niche. The lizards may be a metaphor for the diversity of people in my community.

On our evening walks around the neighborhood, we observed our neighbors. Some of them were walking alone, some in couples, and a few as families. Young couples pushed strollers and older folks just strolled. Some rode bicycles. A few drove golf carts with music blaring, drinks in hand, and the family dog along for the ride. Rich and poor; young and old; black, white, Asian, and Latino—we were all just people getting on with our lives, clinging to whatever ledge we could find.

26

The 'Joy' of Thanksgiving

Published November 26, 2020

In the Fall of 2020, I found myself back on the wagon—the mule wagon, that is. I was on a new property, and it had been nearly a year since my last hunt, so I had to get reacquainted with my mules, Mike and Ike. My faithful old retriever Joy was semi-retired, but some new, young English cockers were ready to take her place next to me on the wagon. Shep and Millie worked one day, and Brody worked the next with Joy along for the ride. We were all a bit rusty.

After seven months, I was a bit apprehensive about climbing back on the wagon. I had grown accustomed to my COVID-induced isolation, keeping several facemasks in my car, and facing plexiglass shields in the stores. But, I rationalized, I drove for a family and their guests, not the general public. Being outdoors and somewhat isolated on my wagon seat seemed safe enough for me. Hunting, like golf, is an easily distanced outdoor sport. Hunters don't need to wear masks while shooting and we greeted with gloved fist-bumps.

The property where I hunted those days was new to quail hunting. It was ideal quail habitat—wide-open pine-savanna—and it was burned that spring for the first time in years. The results were astonishing. I wish I could have identified the wildflowers I saw. The fields were a sea of color, mostly in yellow and orange, interspersed with some blues. It was the first cool snap. The quail were flying like mad and even the best shooters were having trouble drawing a bead. I, too, had my challenges when Mike and Ike lost their patience midway through the afternoon and began acting up.

Actually, my struggles began early in the day when I needed help throwing the heavy harnesses across the head-high backs of the mules. Then, when loading them into the trailer, I forgot to let go of their bridles and got dragged inside sandwiched between two, thousand-pound mules. The only member of the hunt that did not struggle that day was our retriever, Joy.

Joy was solid brown—known as "liver" color—and was about fifteen years old, which was ancient for a working dog. She was covered in wart-like skin tags, had an ominous lump growing on her left side, and was nearly deaf. Joy was so good at her job that she was never clipped to the wagon, but those days when her name was called from the field, she couldn't hear the call, anyway. I needed to give her a pat on the head and tell her it was time to go.

Joy was always watching the action. When she saw the hunters kicking about in the underbrush looking for a downed bird, she was ready to go—unlike Brody, her three-year-old wagon-mate. Brody was a handsome, athletic, brown and white cocker and a veteran of last year's hunt. He knew his job—or so we thought.

The first time he was called to find a bird, I unclipped him and he bounded down the steps. But when he reached the ground and turned to the front of the wagon, he froze. He appeared to be surprised at the knot of horses and mules in front of him. Or perhaps he forgot what he was supposed to do once he was on the ground. That happens to me more often than I care to admit—like when I walk into a room and wonder why I went in there.

Whatever the reason, Brody stood for a moment then turned and bounded back up on the wagon. Chris, the guide, called as I attempted to push him off, but Brody wasn't having it. The hunters continued to look for the bird and everyone grew impatient, so Chris had to make the call.

"JOY!"

All thoughts of an aging retriever faded from our minds as the old girl sprang from the wagon. She navigated the lanes to where the hunters waited and found the missing quail in no time. But when she brought her treasure back, she faced one final indignity. She was not spry enough to leap onto the wagon. She had to be lifted to the steps by one of the guides so she could drop the bird in my hand and return her attention to the field. Joy was thankful, it appeared, to be back in the game. The rest of the day's hunt was hers.

It seems fitting that Thanksgiving coincides with hunting season. Hunting has been an essential part of Thanksgiving since the Pilgrims sat down with the Wampanoags in 1621. And we know from firsthand accounts that "wild fowl" was on the menu. I wonder if that included the northern bobwhite quail.

Today, we tend to replace wild game and the bounty of the harvest with huge, pen-raised frozen turkeys and a table-full of canned vegetables. But in many parts of the country—like South Georgia—where Thanksgiving coincides with hunting season, people still include wild game and fowl on the menu. In the rural south, there is more to Thanksgiving than gorging ourselves and watching football. There are the hunt and the harvest that precede the meal.

I wasn't raised as a hunter. I never spent cool, fall mornings in the woods with my dad. I came late to the party. But even though I am old, I still appreciated the hunting experience as much as Joy seemed to. I was grateful, on that Thanksgiving holiday, to be back in the game because even though Joy and I may have needed a little help from time to time, we could still get the job done.

So, I figured, prop me up on the wagon and hand me the reins. I'll guide the mules through the woods. And when you call me for Thanksgiving dinner, shout a little louder and give me a pat on the head. I'll take it from there—if I can remember why I came into the room.

27

A Sign of the Times

Published January 8, 2021

Yard signs are big business these days. Gone are the days when a sign in someone's yard meant their house was for sale. These days, signs are posted all over my neighborhood. They advertise pest control, irrigation, roofing, swimming pool maintenance, and tree removal. My neighbors want me to know what school they support, that *Black Lives Matter*, and that I should *Back the Blue*. Lately, these signs have revealed our political leanings. During the election campaign, supporters of President Trump posted enthusiastic displays with flags and whirligigs while Biden folks seemed more subdued, often with handmade signs.

And just when I thought the endless political season was over, we Georgians were treated to a runoff campaign for two U.S. Senate seats. The only positive note was that the four people who were campaigning seemed to have combined their efforts, much like the presidential races. On the Republican side, we had the Loeffler-Perdue "ticket" and for the Democrats, I saw yard signs for Warnock-Ossoff. Maybe that meant fewer yard signs and fewer TV and radio commercials. That election season couldn't end too soon for me. The campaign ads had become offensive and insulting—and not just for the candidates.

Human beings are tribal animals and Americans may be the most tribal of all. We fly our flags, display our school colors, and support our state and local sports teams. Actually "support" is too mild a word. Love and hate seem more appropriate when it comes to college athletics. Our neighborhood watch groups keep an eye on any outsiders who might wander into our neighborhoods. Many Americans, it seems, want to keep people who don't look like us off our streets or foreigners from coming to our country and "taking our jobs." Even though these immigrants are taking jobs no one else wants. It is hard to find people who want to clean motel rooms or pick tomatoes. I appreciate immigrants who want to work hard and get ahead. My sentiments are shared by some folks in Louisville, Kentucky. On a recent visit there, I saw numerous yard signs that said: *No matter where you are from, we're glad you're our neighbor.* It was printed in three languages.

Many of the yard signs I see suggest we are a bitterly divided country. It is no longer good enough to be an American. We must declare a party allegiance. Am I a Republican or a Democrat, a conservative or a liberal? I would like to be neither or perhaps both. I would like my government to rule by common sense and compromise—something that might approach the common good. I am a middle of the road kind of guy who is tired of the prevailing "my way or the highway" attitude. I could support a moderate Republican or a moderate Democrat if there were any of them in existence.

I am okay with my neighbors displaying *Black Lives Matter* signs. While it is true that all lives matter, we don't need a sign to remind us that white lives matter. I grew up in the segregated South at a time when the only lives that seemed to matter were white lives. I will support the Black Lives Matter movement until *all* lives really do matter.

I don't have any signs in my yard even though I support Georgia football and Braves baseball. If I am paying a company to service my air conditioner or to cut my trees then I think they should pay me for advertising their business with a sign in my yard. All these yard signs are visual pollution to me. There should be limits—like one sign per yard and a one-month time limit per sign. And if you place a sign advertising your candidate or your yard sale on a street corner, you should be fined if you don't remove it when the election or the event is over.

On my recent visit to Kentucky, I saw yard signs that proclaimed: *Black lives matter, women's rights are human rights, immigrants make America great, science is real, and kindness is everything.* In many cases, all these sentiments were on a single sign. That is a sign I might place in my yard, although I have not seen any signs that cover an important segment of our population. To my sign, I would need to add ***be kind to animals***. Their lives matter, too.

28

Dogs on the Hunt

Published February 3, 2021

When the last of our dogs died of natural causes a few years ago, we decided to take a break from dog ownership for a while. Aging parents and the resulting need for spur-of-the-moment travel was the primary reason. I miss having a dog around and will someday invite one or two back into my home but, in the meantime, I have a marvelous substitute—a grand-dog. Our son in Atlanta acquired a golden retriever puppy a few years ago and Libby has grown up and become part of the family. His wife also brought a dog to our family—a pint-sized cocker spaniel named Alice. What a pair Alice and Libby make.

According to the American Kennel Club (AKC), the golden retriever is an exuberant gundog that was developed as a breed in Scotland in the mid-1800s. They are serious laborers at hunting and field work, a breed built to find and retrieve waterfowl. The cocker spaniel, on the other hand, is a compact sporting dog that is famous the world over for the ability to find, flush, and retrieve gamebirds. The contrasting characteristics of these two breeds became apparent to me on a walk. Libby, the retriever, walked with her head up and nose twitching as she carefully watched the world around her. Alice, on the other hand, kept her nose to the ground, seemingly oblivious to anything that didn't have a smell.

Observing how these two dogs interact with the world around them helped me appreciate the diversity of dogs and how we have shaped and bred dogs to be much more than just pets and companions. Dogs are our partners at a variety of jobs, and I have a soft spot for working dogs.

I recently learned that we share our world with about a billion dogs. We have around seventy-five million in the United States, alone. Dogs evolved from an ancestor of the gray wolf, which has been around for three-hundred thousand years. But how did we get to the modern dog from this ruthless carnivore?

The earliest dogs appeared about fifteen thousand years ago when humans began displacing Neanderthals in northern Europe and Asia. But the explosion of diversity in shape and size only occurred about two hundred years ago with a breeding craze in Europe and the advent of kennel clubs in the 1800s. Dogs are great companions and have been bred to hunt, herd, and protect. But they can also learn an astonishing variety of tasks. They assist us in therapy, in search and rescue, in policing, and even in war.

Most surprising to me is the recent speculation that humans did not domesticate wolves. Wolves domesticated themselves. They accomplished this by staying in proximity to human settlements, scavenging our leftovers, and adapting to our ways over generations. Wolves evolved into dogs and became hunting companions that were a perfect complement to humans. Dogs were the chasers, and humans were the finishers. We both shared the spoils of the hunt.

At this point, I should confess that Libby and Alice will probably never share in the spoils of any hunts. Both are house dogs. They are pets that provide companionship. But they also represent the diverse traits and abilities that we humans have shaped into working partnerships.

For thousands of years, humans have bred dogs for specific traits. As humans became more sophisticated, so did their dogs. Eventually, specific breeds of dogs emerged, custom-bred to suit the breeders' local needs and circumstances. Huge mastiff types were bred as guard dogs and warriors. Sleek greyhound types were bred to chase fleet-footed prey.

So, then, when is a breed a breed and not just a type of dog? The simplest way to define a breed, according to the AKC, is to say it always *breeds true*. Breeding a purebred golden retriever to another purebred golden retriever will always produce golden retriever puppies. The

AKC recognizes hundreds of breeds and classes them into eight or nine groups. These groups include sporting dogs, herding dogs, hounds, terriers, and more.

Most of the dogs I have owned have been mutts. They were rescued from some animal shelter. But I do appreciate dogs that were bred for a specific purpose. When I drove the mule wagon, I had a ringside seat to some of the most enthusiastic sporting dogs on the planet—the pointers, which the AKC calls "the unquestioned aristocrats of the sporting world," and the English cockers, the champions of *find, flush, and retrieve.*

Millie and Shep were a couple of English cockers that rode with me during my last years on the wagon. When they were in their first year on the wagon and still in training, they picked up the art of finding birds with amazing quickness. It must have been in their genes. They helped me appreciate the talent of Joy, my original wagon-dog, who died at the age of fifteen. Unlike Joy, who would never leave until called, these young dogs had to be clipped to the wagon, so they didn't rush out and spoil the hunt. And when they did hunt, Joy could have taught them a thing or two.

I recall one cold January morning several years earlier when we were hunting with Joy on the wagon near a water-filled low area called a "bottom." When one of the birds fell in the middle of that bottom in a foot or two of water I marked where it splashed down, but assumed it was lost. Nobody was likely to wade out into the freezing water to retrieve that bird.

The hunter and guide gathered at the water's edge to gaze out to their lost quarry and to my great surprise the guide turned back to the wagon and called for Joy. The excited cocker who was in her prime had been watching intently. She scrambled down off the wagon without hesitation to join the hunters, but she did not stop at the water's edge. She blew past the men, jumped into the water, and splashed out to where the bird had fallen. A few moments later, she was back on the wagon soaking wet with a quail dangling from her mouth and muddy ice-water dripping all over my seat.

Our thirty-pound cocker had no trouble bounding through the water to retrieve a six-ounce quail. But what if we were hunting waterfowl? Joy couldn't possibly retrieve a three-pound mallard. That would be a job for a big dog like Libby, my son's golden retriever—a breed built to find and retrieve waterfowl. Libby, however, is not a trained hunting dog and will not be swimming after any downed ducks. But I do know another Porter dog that can retrieve—my nephew Jared's yellow Labrador retriever. Penny lives up to her AKC description as "an enthusiastic athlete that requires lots of exercise, like swimming and marathon games of fetch to keep physically and mentally fit."

I thought of Penny when I saw Joy go after the quail that fell in the water. Penny's skill at marking birds was evident at just one year of age, when Jared and Penny were hunting the greater white-fronted goose (or specklebelly) during a trip to Louisiana. The specklebelly is a large species that weighs in at more than five pounds. Jared managed to hit a bird, but it sailed a good two-hundred yards.

"Penny marked it the whole way," Jared told me, "And when I sent her after it, she disappeared over a levee. A minute later back she came, toting a goose that looked as big as she was."

Jared is an avid outdoorsman and hunter who knew he wanted a hunting dog that had the drive to hunt but that could also live inside as a companion dog. He and his wife acquired Penny about four years ago from a breeder who specializes in hunting retrievers. Penny apparently inherited all the right traits because her drive to hunt is intense.

I don't see that drive in all the young cockers that are trained on my wagon. Though they all have the same natural instincts, some dogs like Shep and Millie show interest in the hunt and love to find birds. Others are content to lick themselves and try to climb into my lap. These dogs end up going home to some family. A few lucky dogs, like Penny, get to be family dogs and hunters.

"I think people who see her lounging around our house and yard in a pink collar," Jared told me, "Would be surprised to know that she relishes chasing down geese at a hundred yards. I do look at [her] like two different dogs, a spoiled house pet, and an attentive and driven field dog."

When I began my retirement career as a wagon driver, part of the morning routine was driving the wagon to the kennel to load all the dogs—all the dogs, that is, except Joy. Joy did not sleep at the kennel during hunting season. She slept on the seat of the wagon. She was there every morning when I arrived, curled up on the blanket I had prepared the evening before. She refused to be lured into the kennel or the barn on cold nights, so we had to rig up makeshift tents and heat lamps. I'm not sure how or why the practice began, but that's just the way it was. Joy was about as pure a hunting dog as I ever saw. I don't believe she would have been happy sleeping on someone's couch. Penny the Labrador retriever, on the other hand, seems to enjoy both worlds. She sleeps in a comfortable house but is a formidable hunting dog.

Like most dogs, Penny arrived with her hunting instincts preloaded. At just a couple of months old, she was bounding after and retrieving her stuffed penguin in the house. Soon after, she was introduced to bumpers, which are plastic or rubber dummies that are used to train retrievers. She quickly learned how to "heel," or stand at the trainer's hip, and to wait until her name was called to retrieve the bumper. Jared hunts out of a wide kayak known as a layout boat, so Penny had to learn where to sit and how to jump back in the boat after she retrieves a duck.

A hunting dog has a lot to learn and will thrive on training and practice, so I wonder if there is a trade-off by having a hunting dog live in the house. Jared wonders about that, too. Perhaps, he suggests, if he were stricter or "kept it more businesslike," Penny would be even better in the field. But her being a mix of family dog and gun dog is what he and his wife want. So, Penny must make up for her lack of intense training with some instinct and a good bit of skill. And one of the best illustrations of her combination of instinct and skill was illustrated on one recent trip.

"Wood ducks were the main bird we hunted," Jared recalls, "and we had to work hard to sometimes scratch out one or two. This day ended up being especially noteworthy because one duck actually dove, and Penny went under as well and came up with it. That's definitely not a trained skill!"

As a dog owner, it is useful for me to know what makes my dog happy. Dogs like Libby and Penny are retrievers, so they want to, well, retrieve. Penny is an expert at retrieving ducks from water-filled swamps while Libby is constantly trying to sneak sticks into the house after a walk. Cockers like Millie, Shep, and even Alice, will enjoy an opportunity to take their time and have a good sniff around their world.

And which of these hunting dogs have it best? My son's dogs Libby and Alice, who live a life of ease and comfort; Joy, who slept on a wagon seat and knew nothing but the hunt; or Penny, who appears to have the best of both worlds? There is no right answer to this. Dogs are our original hunting companions—our oldest canine partners. They just want to be with us, doing what we do.

Come to think of it, these hunting dogs are a little bit like me. I love the hunt and am attentive when on the wagon—perhaps because people are waving loaded shotguns in my direction—but I also enjoy stretching out on the couch after the hunt like a spoiled house pet. And, contrary to what my wife says, I require very little training.

29

The Search for a Fitting Final Legacy

Published March 10, 2021

Anyone who knows me knows I like to write. There is just something about the creative process that I find satisfying—finding the right word, the perfect turn of phrase, the rhythm of the story. During our 2020 COVID isolation I finished writing a memoir and a novel—my third and fourth books—but that 74,000-word novel nearly did me in. It was like running a marathon.

Thirty years ago, I fancied myself a woodcarver. I liked to create animals and accumulated quite a collection of wooden birds, mammals, and reptiles. In the early 1990s, I made a small Noah's Ark for my wife as a Christmas present. My plan was to give her two tiny new animals every year thereafter. I enlisted our three-year-old son Ian and we carved and painted the animals together. We amassed a collection many zoos would be proud of, from zebras to hummingbirds and elephants to meerkats. We finally stopped the two-decade-old tradition when he was grown. In fact, I stopped carving altogether. I had run out of room to store all my carvings and ran out of friends and relatives to fob them off on. That's when I turned to writing.

Creativity can take many forms, as we observed during the past pandemic shutdowns. My wife is an accomplished painter. She spent some of her time in lockdown making art. Musicians who couldn't play their instruments in a concert hall, played for their neighbors from the balcony. Baking supplies were scarce because folks were making cakes. Australians amused themselves by dressing up in costumes for their only outing of the week, taking out the garbage (or, as they call it, "the wheelie bin").

One of the things that struck me during the pandemic creativity-binge was how much of our creativity is drawn out by bringing joy to others. Creativity comes from a combination of talent and enjoyment of the process, and it thrives in the presence of an appreciative audience. I enjoy writing articles, but I also like it when people stop me in the grocery store to tell me how much they like reading them. Those cooped-up musicians in Italy who were playing Bach from their balconies probably listened carefully for the smattering of applause from the canyon of high-rise apartments around them.

Many of us have creative energy we scarcely recognize. We photograph, we bake, we write, we start a home-grown business, we even dress up like a dinosaur to take out the trash. It is part of the human spirit. And if you don't know how to do something, you can take some lessons or you can YouTube it. That's how I learned how to repair my lawnmower, refinish my wooden staircase, and change the cabin air filter in my 2011 Nissan Rogue. Creativity takes many forms, especially if you can't afford to pay someone else to do something.

Creativity is good for the soul, and it runs in my family. My dad was a plasterer by trade but always worked with his hands. He grew plants, created a backyard smokehouse, designed a rockscape waterfall, worked on cars, and built a garage addition on our house. My own creativity runs in so many directions that I sometimes experience a kind of creative ADHD.

I created built-in bookshelves in my last three homes and a fireplace mantle in our current home. My wife and I constructed a shed, a fire pit, and dug a goldfish pond with a fountain. When Hurricane Michael destroyed our swimming pool, we filled it in and turned the space into a formal garden—complete with handmade steppingstones and a giant urn bubbler. In the last couple of months, I made a new furniture cabinet for the back porch and a set of giant Jenga blocks for my grandchildren.

Long before the pandemic, my father-in-law's neighbors in Louisville, Kentucky let loose their creativity by turning an old tree stump at the edge of their yard into a gnome home. It was complete with a roof, doors, windows, and several gnomes doing chores around the *gnome-stead*. And the scene changes with the seasons and holidays. People were constantly stopping to admire the gnomes and take their pictures. I am sure that was the goal of the Powells when they created this inspired diorama.

Now that my father-in-law has passed away, my wife is repaying the help and kindness the Powells provided him by doing a painting of that gnome home for them. Her creativity has been unleashed by theirs and will likely bring them joy for years to come.

In the 1980s, early in my wood-carving years, I answered an ad in the newspaper from someone selling some woodworking tools. I was in the market for some chisels. When I arrived at the home of the seller, I was met by a woman who turned out to be the widow of a woodcarver who had recently passed away. She escorted me to his workshop where I picked out a few chisels from his collection. But as I self-consciously sorted through a dead man's tool collection, I came face to face with an uncomfortable reality. Perched on the man's work bench was a life-sized wood carving of a great blue heron. It was unfinished and still emerging from a block of wood, but it had a well-defined beak, head, and neck. It was beautifully done, and I found it at once humbling in its quality and inspiring in its beauty. Now, as I look back on that experience after nearly four decades, I see another message. That man was working on that bird right up until the end. His unfinished work left a piece of him behind for us to admire—a kind of unintended legacy in wood, still bringing joy to others. That is what creativity is all about.

That is what I hope for myself. I want to leave an unfinished work, whether it be a carving, a piece of furniture, or one of these articles. I want to bring pleasure to others by creating right up until the end. I do have an idea for another book. Or maybe I'll dust off my chisels and make another pair of animals for the ark. But no, I need a new challenge—something I've never tried before. Maybe I'll make a home for the gnomes that live in my garden. There are seven of the white-bearded little guys. I talk to them sometimes, one old man to another. Surely, I didn't imagine their faint voices early in the morning singing, "Heigh-Ho, Heigh-Ho, it's off to work we go." Or maybe that final project is nearer than I thought.

30

At Home with the Gnomes

Published July 8, 2021

My wife is particular about the creatures that occupy her garden. Birds of all types are welcome. The neighbor's cat is not. Turtles that munch on clover are welcome. Deer that mow down her daylilies are not. This even extends to inanimate objects. Frogs live in our pond and frog figurines surround it. But not all figurines are allowed. We only have frogs in natural poses. You won't find any frogs playing banjos in our garden.

And then there are the gnomes. There is nothing natural about them, but they have somehow multiplied over the years and lurk in several corners of the garden. We have large ones and small ones, some painted and some *au naturel* (not naked, just unpainted). We have so many of them, they needed a place to live. That's why I finally completed that gnome home I have been promising to make.

According to the *New World Encyclopedia*, a gnome is a type of legendary creature that lives in dark places in the depths of forests and, more recently, in gardens. Modern traditions portray gnomes as small, old men wearing pointed hats. But, historically, the term "gnome" includes a variety of creatures. Goblins, for example, come out of German and British folklore and are usually described as troublemakers as opposed to the more benevolent fairy. Elves are from Norse mythology and leprechauns are diminutive supernatural beings in Irish folklore, usually depicted as small, bearded men wearing a coat and hat.

The earliest appearance of gnome-like statues was the representation of gods in ancient Roman gardens. It is believed that the very first contemporary garden gnome (with its iconic red hat), was made in Germany and brought to England in the 1840s. Gnomes have been a presence in the English garden—and later in North America—ever since.

The "traveling gnome" was introduced in the 1970s and became widely popular during the 1990s when people began stealing gnomes and taking them traveling. Thieves usually sent photographs of the gnomes to the owners, showing them that their minions were safe and sound, and enjoying their newly gained freedom and independence. Over time, the prank became popular on a global scale, with many cases of stolen traveling garden gnomes appearing in photographs in front of famous landmarks worldwide. Today, we even see a gnome front man with a cute British accent for a well-known travel website.

Most gnomes—whether they be satyrs, pans, dryads, elves, brownies, or goblins—hoard treasure and interact mischievously or even harmfully with humans. But some gnomes, it is said, are helpful to plants and animals. Judging by my wife's success in her garden, those are the ones that live with us.

Our gnomes are only active after dark and appear to come inside the house on occasion. Some people have ghosts or poltergeists. We have gnomes. Our gnomes rank somewhere between mischievous leprechauns and benevolent fairies. They nurtured us through the pandemic by giving us a sense of peace and calm. They help my wife with her plants in the garden, nudge both of us to go on long walks, and stir up gentle breezes to tickle the wind chimes during my afternoon naps on the porch.

On the other hand, when my wife comes into the room and asks me to call her cell phone so she can locate it, I'm pretty sure the gnomes have hidden it. When we are watching TV on a clear, calm evening and the electricity goes off—just long enough to force a reset of all the clocks and electronics—that is classic gnome behavior. And recently, when we were headed out for our evening walk and discovered that a box turtle had somehow clambered up a small step and plopped into the fishpond—well, there is only one explanation for that.

Early humans created gnome-like creatures to explain the unexplainable. Every culture, it seems, has a version so there must be something to it. As a Christian, I see God's handiwork in my life, which might include sending the gnomes as his angels. That is why I built the gnome home. It not only looks nice nestled in the garden, but it also makes our little buddies feel welcome and gives them a place to call home. Maybe now they will spend more time in their own yard and less time hiding phones and dropping turtles into our fishpond.

31

Let the Walking Man Walk

Published August 23, 2021

"I have met with but one or two persons in the course of my life," Henry David Thoreau wrote, "who understood the art of walking." His 1862 article in the *Atlantic* magazine was titled, appropriately enough, "Walking." A little over a hundred years later, singer / songwriter James Taylor took up the subject in a song that has become my anthem—"The Walking Man." Now, here I am in what might be called my twilight years trying to be James Taylor's walking man while understanding Thoreau's art of walking. Some days, when my arthritis is acting up, I feel more like the aching man. But James Taylor's lyric usually nudges me out the door—"While any other man stops and talks, the walking man walks."

I look forward to my morning walk. It is part of my daily ritual along with getting dressed, having a cup of coffee, and brushing my teeth. Some days are better than others. It depends on the weather, my daily schedule of chores and errands, and how my worn-out old body feels. I am fortunate that I am physically able to walk, that I have a safe neighborhood in which to do it, and I have a family heritage of walking.

I usually walk alone listening to a podcast on my headphones. That is when I do my best thinking. I wrote this article in my head while on one of my walks. I try to walk through fatigue and injury, in all types of weather, dodging cars, lawn service trailers parked in the street, and the occasional dog running loose. I also enjoy walking with my wife. We talk more on our walks than we do when we are busy at home. It is, I think, good for our marriage.

When I began my daily walks, I tried to walk two miles and three miles on alternate days, but I have had to dial back a bit to ease my aching back. Now I try for about two miles a day with a couple of days off each week.

I obviously enjoy walking, or I wouldn't do it. It is good exercise. I see interesting scenery, including birds and wildlife. And I get to be a nosy neighbor as I casually inspect houses and yards. Karen and I have a good time with this. *When are they going to mow their lawn? Why did they paint their house that color?* And, a pet peeve, *Why is that car parked on the lawn and not in the driveway? And why has it not moved in over a week?*

I regularly encounter fellow walkers. These include the serious walkers (fast pace, head down, arms pumping); the strollers (Thoreau calls them saunterers); the buddy walkers locked in conversation as they go; the cell-phone talkers; the dog walkers; and the half dozen walkers on the golf course who walk up and down the fairway side by side in a line. My wife and I call them the crime scene finger-tip search team.

I come from a long line of walkers, although it skipped a generation with my parents. They didn't walk much, but my grandparents sure did. When my brothers and I spent weekends with Grandma Porter, she walked us all over St. Petersburg, Florida. We walked to the grocery store and drug store when she needed supplies. We walked to the ice cream shop after dinner. When she needed to go downtown, she walked us four blocks to the bus stop on Sixteenth Street. When the bus dropped us downtown in Williams Park, we walked through the park to Maas Brothers Department store, down to the pier, and other destinations as needed. Then it was back to the park to catch the bus home. It wasn't like she couldn't get a ride in someone's car. She didn't want a ride. She had her own two feet—and the city bus.

It is hard to imagine, but there was a time when exercise wasn't a thing. Grandma Porter didn't walk because it was good for her health. She wasn't worried about her cardio workout or how many steps she got in. She was just a walker.

In his essay on walking, Thoreau said, "I cannot preserve my health and spirits, unless I spend four hours a day at least—and it is commonly more than that—sauntering through the woods and over the hills and fields, absolutely free from all worldly engagements."

Four hours is a heck of a walk, but he only walked in the fields, forests, and woods. And he embraced the idea of sauntering, so he probably stopped frequently to sit on a log and contemplate nature. Thoreau would have laughed at my pathetic excuse for a walk. I am out for less than an hour and the only wildlife I see are the squirrels, rabbits, and birds that peer at me from my neighbors' lawns.

A real walk, according to Thoreau, is when "you are ready to leave father and mother, and brother and sister, and wife and child and friends, and never see them again—if you have paid your debts, and made your will, and settled all your affairs, and are a free man—then you are ready for a walk."

Good grief. Who can measure up to that? The only thing that gives me hope is that he also said, "[Walking] comes only by the grace of God. It requires a direct dispensation from Heaven to become a walker. You must be born into the family of walkers."

There, I do have some "street creds." I do come from a family of walkers, and I have Grandma Porter's dispensation. So, I will continue my daily walks with Thoreau's inspiration in my heart and James Taylor's anthem in my head. *Who is this walking man?*

32

The Right to Roam...
Good for the Soul

Published September 28, 2021

In the Cattail Creek community outside Burnsville, North Carolina it was known as "the Mt. Mitchell Hike." My wife Karen and I did it twice. It was a four-hour trek from the top of Mt. Mitchell, the highest point east of the Mississippi at 6,684 feet, down the northwest side of the mountain to my Mom and Dad's cabin on Deep Gap Road. The trail—and I use that term loosely—meandered down steep grades and switchbacks with a drop in elevation of about two thousand feet. There were no signs to point the way, so we needed a guide.

 The first couple of hours walking from the Mt. Mitchell peak took us along the ridge of the Black Mountains, through small valleys and up to new peaks. We passed over Big Tom, Balsam Cone, Cattail Peak, and Potato Hill. We began our two-thousand-foot descent at a place called Deep Gap and were soon out of the State Park and onto private property. I never saw any signs, but I am pretty sure we were trespassing for the rest of our hike. We never met any resistance from landowners, but if we had been in parts of Western Europe, we would have been protected by something called the Right to Roam.

 In countries like Scotland, Finland, Iceland, Norway, Sweden, and Switzerland, the freedom to roam the countryside has been written into specific laws. The right to roam is considered so important to the health and mental well-being of these nations, that it supersedes that peculiarly American concept of private property—a concept that is, by nature, exclusive.

In Europe, the right to enter and walk through a person's property does not include any economic activities like hunting or logging nor does it allow any disruptive activities like building fires and driving off-road vehicles. Instead, every person has a right to explore these vast open spaces; to sleep there; to kayak, swim, and climb; and to ride horses and bicycles. Roamers are even accommodated by landowners with self-closing rambler gates, kissing gates, and climbable stile gates which allow people but not livestock to pass through.

This right, however, is contingent on adhering to a strict set of responsibilities. These are simple, basic rules on how to behave in the countryside in such a way that you neither interrupt the function of a working, agricultural landscape, nor damage the ecology of where you roam. When children grow up in these countries, experiencing nature and learning the code in practical terms, these codes become second nature—part of a wider understanding of how humans should interact with nature and with each other.

The combination of rights and responsibilities creates a relationship with the natural world in which nature is no longer presented like some abstract museum piece, to be observed from afar behind a line of barbed wire. Instead, it becomes a multi-sensory tangible experience with unique smells, sounds, and sights. The right to roam ensures that the government actively encourages people to go outside. It removes any sense that being in nature is a criminal activity and creates an inherent connection with nature. Right to roamers feel that nature should be accessible for all, and rights of access should be extended to give more people in towns and cities easy access to nature.

The closest thing to a right to roam in this country is our "rails to trails" projects. Americans, it appears, aren't much for walking long distances. So, most of our attention goes to bicycle trails. In Tallahassee, people can ride or walk the twenty-one miles down to the picturesque waterfront village of St. Marks. The Swamp Rabbit Trail in Greenville, South Carolina is a twenty-two-mile multi-use (walking and bicycling) greenway that follows the banks of the Reedy River. And in Atlanta, people have multiple options including the Beltline and the sixty-mile Silver Comet trail. In America, if we want to "ramble," we need to go to a park, a nature preserve, or an arrow-straight, paved, mini-roadway where we must give way to a steady stream of bicycles.

The Mt. Mitchell hike was a true ramble. We walked along overgrown roadbeds, scrambled down steep grades, and stepped across clear mountain streams. Rambling like that is good for the soul and creates an inherent connection with nature. I need to do it more often.

As far as I know, we had no right to wander down the side of Mt. Mitchell. Once we left the park boundary, we had no legal authority to cross private property without the owners' permission. We just did it. In Europe, we would have been protected by law. Here in the United States, who knows what might have happened in the back woods of the Appalachian wilderness. If we had made T-shirts for our hike, the front would have featured something about Mt. Mitchell and it being the highest elevation east of the Mississippi. But the back of the shirt might have recalled the 1972 movie Deliverance and read, "Walk faster. I think I hear banjo music."

33

The Matriarch—
A Mother's Day Tribute

Published May 14, 2023

We faced each other like a couple of gunslingers at high noon. I was a young zookeeper, armed with a three-foot-long stick called a bull hook. My opponent brought his pair of impressive ivory tusks and six-thousand-pounds of bulk. Bwana stood about twenty yards away, facing me with his trunk up and his ears fanned out in a threat display. He was a nine-year-old male African elephant, and he was testing me to see who was in charge.

If he had been in the wild, there would have been no doubt who was boss. It would have been his mother. That's because wild African elephants live in a matriarchal society—a world that is dominated by the females.

A mother elephant will usually try to set an unruly youngster right with a gentle nudge in the right direction or, if that doesn't work, a sharp slap with her trunk. And when a young male like Bwana approaches puberty at ten to twelve years of age, his mother probably won't try to coax him back like I did. At that age, she is more likely to force him out of the herd. Adult males lead solitary lives or live temporarily in a smaller herd with other young bulls until it is time to breed.

Another matriarchal society that some might find surprising is a fearsome, ocean-dwelling creature that hunts in packs, chases seals for sport, and can kill a great white shark. That's right, killer whales are also ruled by their mothers. Killer whales, or Orcas, are the largest member of the dolphin family. They live in female-led pods, where they hunt together and share responsibility for raising the young and taking care of the sick or injured.

Thinking about matriarchal societies seems like a good way to remember my own mother on Mother's Day. She came to motherhood at an early age and took it on with tenacity. She married my father at eighteen and had me a year later. She tragically lost her second child—her only daughter—in childbirth but went on to have three more sons. Perhaps the most remarkable thing about Carol Porter is how unremarkable her story is. But I am glad we set aside a day for me to continue to honor her, even though she would insist she was just doing her job as a mother.

I should honor my wife, too. She may not be my mother, but she is the best mother I know. And her motherly love can even cross species barriers. In the late 1990s, a female gorilla in a zoo at which I worked gave birth but was unable to care for her baby for a while. When zookeepers stepped in to care for the infant, we had to find surrogate mothers to hold the baby on a regular basis and to bottle-feed it around the clock. A group of dedicated volunteers—including my wife—agreed to take turns caring for the infant gorilla until its mother was able to resume her duties.

In fact, I can think of no better example of motherhood in the animal kingdom than the female gorilla. Gorillas live in troops of a few—to a few dozen—members that are led by a dominant, adult, silverback male. When Zoo Atlanta announced the birth of a gorilla, they reported that the infant appeared healthy and strong, was nursing normally, and was receiving appropriate maternal care. I would expect nothing less from a gorilla mom.

Zoo visitors who are fortunate enough to see an infant might note that gorillas are born with an instinctive ability to hold on to their mothers' chests but, in most other respects, they are helpless. Mothers support their babies for the first few months of life but, unlike humans, gorilla mothers seldom allow other gorillas to hold or carry their infants. Babies learn to crawl and ride on their mothers' backs at about three months of age and may continue to ride on their mothers' backs, chests, or legs for three or four years. If we had a Mother's Day for the animal kingdom, mother gorillas would be high on the list of honorees.

We humans are, I suppose, neither matriarchal nor patriarchal—although America seems to be a more gorilla-like patriarchal society. My home growing up was certainly male dominated. My mom was outnumbered by my three brothers, my dad, and me. The toilet seat was always up in our house.

But that's not to say my mom didn't exert her influence. She could, at times, seem as powerful as a hurricane or as gentle as a summer breeze. She could bandage a skinned knee, soothe an injured ego, or send us outside to break a switch off the willow tree so she could use it on our bare behind.

My mom stayed home until my youngest brother was in school then she gave up that quaint notion that the woman's place is in the home. She got a job with Bell Telephone and stayed with them for the rest of her working life.

She died a few years ago and I miss her terribly. I wish I could send her a card or call her on Mother's Day to tell her I love her—and to thank her for not forcing me out of the herd when I reached puberty.

34

The Silverback—
A Father's Day Tribute

Published June 20, 2021

As a young zookeeper at Busch Gardens in the 1970s, I was in awe of him. Hercules was a four-hundred-pound, male gorilla—a silverback. Hercules lived with his mate Megera but, to the best of my knowledge, he never sired any offspring. In those days, we assumed that if you put a male and female gorilla together, nature would take its course. Today, we know that gorillas live in stable family groups numbering from six to thirty animals. Each group is led by one or two mature males that are related to each other, usually a father and one or more of his sons. The sons learn their roles from the silverback. Hercules, however, was taken out of the wild as an infant. He never had the opportunity to learn how to be a father.

I learned how to be a father from my dad. Jim Porter was the silverback of our family. He served in the Army during World War II—a sergeant in the Military Police. After the war, he trained as a plasterer and raised four boys. I was the oldest and worked as his chief laborer. I mixed "mud" when he had a side-job plastering someone's walls. On nights when the mullet were running and he was out throwing his cast net, I carried a five-gallon bucket and swatted mosquitoes in the darkness of some Florida bayou. And I handed him tools when he was under the car repairing the brakes or changing the oil. Like a true silverback, he was quiet and patient—although we did feel the sting of his belt on our bare bottoms from time to time. It may not be fashionable in today's society but in those days our house, like the gorilla family, was a patriarchy.

Gorillas are native to the tropical forests of equatorial Africa. They are the largest of the apes—robust and powerful animals with black skin and hair, and thick powerful bodies. Males are about twice the size of females, weighing in at up to five hundred pounds, and have a saddle of gray or silver hairs on the lower part of the back—hence the term "silverback." The mature silverback makes all the decisions for the troop. He mediates conflicts and he is responsible for their safety and well-being. If the group is attacked, the silverback will protect the group, even at the cost of his own life. But, oddly enough, gorillas don't fight with each other very often. They use ritualized displays that include standing on two legs, running sideways, throwing vegetation, and chest-beating with cupped hands. These impressive displays of agitation usually end with a sidelong glance at the offender that might, in modern parlance, be called a "stink-eye."

The last silverback gorilla I worked with was Akbar. I wrote about him in this excerpt from my memoir, *Lessons from the Zoo: Ten Animals That Changed My Life.*

> One of my first projects as Deputy Director of the Toledo Zoo was the three-million-dollar Kingdom of the Apes area that opened in 1993. Toledo had an impressive collection of great apes that included chimpanzees, orangutans, and two families of gorillas. They lived in a symmetrical, rectangular, 1970s-era facility, with each of the four groups housed in a section that consisted of off-exhibit holding cages, a small indoor glass-fronted dayroom, and a slightly larger open-air outdoor space with a concrete floor. It was all hard-scape—concrete, glass, and steel. No animals had access to grass.
>
> The renovation would improve the holding cages and add an eighteen-thousand-square-foot outdoor Gorilla Meadow and a three-story indoor dayroom. The old outdoor spaces

would have a tall cage structure added to increase the vertical space, and grass would be planted to replace the concrete floor. It was a remarkable transformation, both visually and for the quality of life of the animals.

On Monday, May 17, 1993, I gathered with my colleagues to watch the male gorilla Akbar peer out of the holding area and carefully test the grassy surface of the new Gorilla Meadow exhibit. As soon as he determined it was safe, he allowed females Happy, Malaika, and Elaine to follow. The thrill of seeing the gorillas step into the sunshine was tempered by the concern we felt as Akbar carefully inspected the walls and fences of his new home. Only after he completed his tour of the perimeter and did not find any escape routes did we relax and celebrate our success.

Akbar was raised in a family group, so he knew what it meant to be a silverback. When entering an unfamiliar space, his job was to check out the area to make sure his family would be safe, just like our father always did for us. My brothers and I were not afraid of our dad but, much like the gorilla family, we never had any doubt about who was in charge. I don't remember him throwing any vegetation or beating his chest with cupped hands, but Dad must have used some kind of ritualized threat displays, because he never raised a hand to us in anger. All he had to do was look at us out of the corner of his eye, and we knew we had better listen up. When he said jump, we didn't ask why. We just asked, "how high?" And when we were sitting in his chair, he snapped his fingers, and we moved out of his way.

Jim Porter died in June 2004. I still miss him. My father-in-law (the silverback of my wife's family) died in February 2021. We buried him the Sunday after Father's Day. I miss him, too. For the first time in our lives, my wife and I will not have a silverback to honor on Father's Day. Their passings mark the end of a generation.

A few years ago, my brothers and I traveled back to our hometown of St. Petersburg, Florida for a weekend of golf, a baseball game, and some reminiscing. Dad featured prominently in our collective memory. As I look at the fine men my brothers have become and at how much we love each other and enjoy each other's company, I realize how fortunate we were to have the upbringing we did. Our dad is the strong, male role model that lives on in the hearts and memories of the Porter brothers. We may not have a father to send a card to, but we sure have one to honor on Father's Day. Today's fathers—myself included—are not what they once were. If you have any doubt, watch me snap my fingers when someone is in my chair and see what happens.

35

These 'Flying Primates' Have Something to Crow About

Published May 9, 2021

What is the smartest animal—after humans and primates? Some think it is the animal strutting around my backyard as I write this. I often see him from my upstairs office window, walking in a wide, apparently aimless circle, occasionally stopping to pick at something on the ground. He crosses the patio, walks through the gravel, and back onto the lawn before hopping onto the edge of the birdbath. After a quick drink and another look around, he flies off. He is one of the American crows that comes back to my yard and frequents the birdbath every year in the spring. He is probably nesting somewhere in the area.

When it comes to smarts, that crow is not just another birdbrain. When we think of animals using tools, for example, we often think of primates. But one species of crow that is native to the South Pacific Island of New Caledonia has been called a "flying primate" because of its tool making ability. New Caledonian crows have been observed bending twigs into the shape of a hook to fish bugs out of rotting logs. Researchers suggest that these crows might be the only other animal besides early humans that habitually make hooks in the wild. Other tool-using crows have been seen carrying cups of water to bowls of dry food and breaking off pieces of pinecone to drop on tree climbers near a nest.

And how many animals do you know that hold funerals for their dead? Researchers have observed groups of crows surrounding a recently deceased bird. But the funeral isn't to mourn the dead. The crows are thought to gather together to find out what killed their member.

According to the Cornell University Ornithology Lab, American crows (*Corvus brachyrhynchos*) are common all over North America, ranging from open woods and empty beaches to town centers. They are significantly larger than other black birds and much smaller than ravens, which are found from the northern United States to the Canadian arctic. Their flight style is described as a patient, methodical flapping that is rarely broken up with glides, and their loud caw is unmistakable. Though crows tend to be solitary, they often forage in groups and some crows, especially the yearlings and non-mating adults, live in roosting communities. A group of crows is called a murder. A murder of crows will sometimes band together and chase predators in a behavior called mobbing.

Crows usually feed on the ground and eat almost anything, including earthworms, insects, small animals, seeds, and fruit. They will also pick through garbage and stop on roadways to feed on roadkill. But crows are not just scavengers. They are crafty foragers that sometimes follow other birds to find where their nests are hidden so they can eat the chicks. They have also been observed stealing food from other animals and eating from outdoor dog dishes.

When I see the crows in my neighborhood, I can't tell one from another. They are jet-black and have no distinguishing characteristics. But crows, according to a story on National Public Radio, can recognize and remember me. Wildlife biologists figured this out by conducting experiments using rubber masks. They dressed humans in two masks, one designated a "dangerous" face and another mask as the "neutral" face. Researchers in the dangerous mask trapped and banded individual American crows and then released them. While they were careful not to harm the birds during trapping, it was still a frightening experience for the birds.

To see whether the crows remembered the dangerous face, researchers returned to the area and walked around wearing different masks. When the birds saw the dangerous face, they gave an alarm call and dive-bombed that person. They mostly ignored the neutral face. Researchers even wore the mask upside down to see if the crows could still recognize it. For a brief moment, the crows seemed confused, but when they turned their heads upside down, they sounded an alarm-call.

Even crows that had not been tagged or banded scolded and divebombed the wearer of the dangerous mask, suggesting the crows were learning from their peers that this particular person is dangerous. And, if you need another reason to be nice to crows, researchers suggest that they can remember faces for years.

That crow splashing around while he took a bath in my backyard was so large, he filled the birdbath and splashed most of the water out of the bowl. When he took off in the late afternoon sun, the water glistened on his black feathers, and it sprayed off his flapping wings until he landed in a nearby tree. As I walked out with the garden hose and refilled the birdbath with fresh water, I wondered if he was sizing me up and memorizing my appearance. I gazed up at the crow and gave him a good look at my face. It couldn't hurt to be on the good side of an animal whose group is called a "murder" and who is known to mob his enemies. Besides, since there were no primates around, he was probably the second smartest animal in the neighborhood—which probably wasn't saying much.

36

Why Did It Have to Be Snakes?

Published September 15, 2021

I found it in the garden when I was mowing the lawn. The shed skin of a snake. I saved it for my wife because I knew she would like to show it to the kids at her school. She was indeed pleased, but when she shared our find on social media, her friends were less than impressed.

"OMG," one person said. "No way. Burn the house down."

Others had similar reactions.

"Just had a heart attack," one moaned.

"I would have died," exclaimed another. (This one will remain nameless, but he used to reside at our address.)

Only one person—a fellow teacher—mustered a positive comment. "The kids will love this."

Most people, it appears, agree with Indiana Jones. When he was lowered into an underground chamber in the 1981 film *Raiders of the Lost Ark*, he faced everyone's worst nightmare.

"Snakes," Indy said. "Why did it have to be snakes?"

What is it about snakes?

I spent over forty years managing zoos around the country and handled more than my share of snakes, but I still count myself among those people who suffer from a fear of snakes. It even has a scientific name—*ophidiophobia*. It is a common phobia that can be triggered by a variety of factors that sound familiar to me.

The gulf coast of Florida, where I grew up in the 1960s, was not the thriving metropolis it is today. St. Petersburg was a sleepy retirement village that was carpeted with miles of woodlands and abundant wildlife, including plenty of snakes. Snakes were a part of our lives growing up. We were taught to fear them, especially the ones that could kill us.

But my fear of snakes could also be intrinsic—a part of my DNA. Recent research has found that certain neurons in the brain only respond to snakes. These snake-dedicated neurons may be a legacy of our distant primate past since we share this bias toward snakes with monkeys. When primates evolved some sixty-million years ago, they adapted to living in trees, searching for food at night, and sleeping in the canopy during the day. Snakes creeping through those trees were among their deadliest enemies.

As my career advanced and I began doing education outreach programs on behalf of the various zoos I represented, snakes became a part of my life. It was the creature that audiences loved to hate. People often got up from their seats during my presentations and sometimes even left the room. I handled boa constrictors, ball pythons, and rat snakes. I learned not to recoil at the feel of their muscular legless bodies that were wrapped in smooth, dry leathery skin. I marveled at their forked tongues as they tickled the hairs of my arm, picking up scent molecules to transfer to the "smell" organ inside the roof of their mouth.

I learned to overcome a powerful urge to recoil whenever I reached into a cloth bag to pull out a creature that terrified me. I handled snakes with feigned confidence and regaled my audiences with the importance of snakes to the ecosystem, all while trying to conceal my fear that one of the snakes might turn and bite me.

When we were growing up, if a snake came into our yard our dad dispatched it with a hoe. Later in life, that same man befriended a large black snake that lived in his tool shed. It seems my dad was more concerned with the mice that nibbled his seed packets than a big black snake that ate those mice.

My wife and I are similarly comfortable having non-venomous snakes inhabit our garden. We have seen a large, Eastern garter snake slithering into the iris bed on occasion. We also saw him swimming in the fishpond once. Garter snakes are known to eat fish, but at last count all the goldfish are still there.

Snakes go through a process of sloughing the external layer of skin to allow growth. It is called *ecdysis*, and it occurs every few months, depending on how well they are eating and how fast they are growing. The shed snakeskin I found in our garden was three and a half feet long. According to the *Peterson Field Guide to Reptiles*, garter snakes don't grow that large. So, unless his skin stretched out when he was pulling out of it, the skin must have come from something larger, like perhaps a gray rat snake.

For us, garter snakes and rat snakes are as welcome in our garden as box turtles and lizards. They are harmless residents of a healthy ecosystem. Venomous snakes, on the other hand, will be dispatched without question.

The only concern I have with the snakes in our garden has to do with the location of that shed snakeskin. I found it a few feet from the gnome home. Like the goldfish, I did a head count, and all the little people are present and accounted for. But still, I wonder what kind of fence I could install to keep the snakes away from the gnomes. A rat snake might have a tough time telling a mouse from a three-inch tall gnome—even if he is wearing a pointy, red hat.

37

'Shroomage ... from Portobellos to Death Angels to Dog Vomit

Published November 12, 2021

I am one of a handful of people in my neighborhood who prefers to mow my own lawn. My mower is not a riding mower nor is it self-propelled. It doesn't move unless I push it. That means I know every square foot of my yard intimately and I take pride in the smooth, manicured look of freshly cut grass. It also means I notice anything that mars that perfection—like those mushrooms that appear literally overnight. How is it possible for something to spring up that quickly?

According to the dictionary, mushrooms are *any of the various fleshy fungi of the class Basidiomycetes characteristically having an umbrella-shaped cap borne on a stalk*. The term mushroom typically refers to the edible varieties. The inedible (poisonous) fungi with an umbrella shape are called toadstools.

The umbrella-shaped mushrooms I am thinking about are in the agaric family (*Agaricaceae*). These are the ones that have thin, bladelike gills on the undersurface of the cap that shed spores. They have a cap (pileus) and a stalk (stipe) and emerge from an extensive underground network of threadlike strands called mycelium. That is, apparently, where the magic happens.

The mycelium starts from a spore falling in a favorable spot and producing strands (hyphae) that grow out in all directions, eventually forming a circular mat of underground hyphal threads. Fruiting bodies of some mushrooms occur in arcs or rings called fairy rings that may widen year after year. As long as nourishment is available and temperature and moisture are suitable, a mycelium network can produce a new crop of mushrooms every year during its fruiting season.

The most common varieties of mushroom are probably the ones we find in the grocery store—especially the white or button mushrooms (*Agaricus bisporus*). I purchased an eight-ounce package last week for my slow-cooker beef stew. They were in the produce section next to a variety of other edible mushrooms. After a little research, I discovered that those cremini mushrooms and portobello mushrooms on the next shelf are the same species as the button mushrooms, but at different stages of development. One reference says that if the button mushrooms are at the toddler stage, then creminis are the teenagers, and portobellos are adults.

But what about all the varieties I see around the neighborhood, especially the ones that spring up in my freshly mowed lawn? Well, there are really too many to count and many of them aren't actually mushrooms. They are probably fungi—and they have some pretty colorful names.

Among these are hedgehog mushrooms, which have teeth, spines, or warts on the undersurface of the cap, and club fungi with their shrublike, clublike, or coral-like growth habits. One club fungus, the cauliflower fungus, has flattened clustered branches that lie close together, giving the appearance of the vegetable cauliflower.

The morels are among the most desired wild mushrooms in the world. They are prized for their flavor, texture, and unique appearance, and are popularly included with the true mushrooms because of their shape and fleshy structure. They resemble a deeply folded or pitted conelike sponge at the top of a hollow stem.

The state of Georgia hosts some colorfully descriptive fungi that may be some of the varieties I see around my neighborhood. Wood ear mushrooms, a type of jelly fungus, have earlike shapes and prefer decayed logs and moist areas. Lacquered-shelf fungi grow on decaying hardwood trunks and brown rot fungi consume cellulose in rotting wood. Parasitic shoestring mushrooms grow on hardwoods and conifers and form dark shoestring-like strands under tree bark. One show-stopping fungus is a slime mold called "dog vomit" because of its vibrant yellow-orange hue and its creeping growth.

Georgia has some edible varieties of mushroom, like the chanterelles, but the only mushrooms I eat are the ones from the grocery store. I don't want to take a chance on picking the wrong thing in the wild, like the one called the sickener mushroom. It has a brilliant red cap and thick white stalk with many white, close gills and, as the name implies, it can make you sick. And how about one called the "death angel" mushroom. This one displays a striking white cap and stalk with pure white gills underneath the cap and when eaten can lead to—well, death.

The only wild mushroom I have ever knowingly eaten were the ones my dad grew. They were shitake mushrooms that sprouted from four-foot-long, maple logs leaning up in the shade at the back of his cabin in the North Carolina mountains.

The shitake (*Lentinula edoides*) is a common edible variety of mushroom that is related to the button mushroom but in a different family. Shitakes are native to Southeast Asia and have been harvested for centuries in the warm, moist hardwood forests of China and Japan. They sprout from the decaying wood of deciduous trees like chestnut, oak, and sweetgum and are available in my grocery store.

My dad's spores arrived by mail in a small plastic bag. They were a pressed sawdust product that had been infused with spores and molded into one-inch-long plugs that fit neatly into a quarter-inch, round hole. My brothers and I were charged with drilling hundreds of holes into a pile of four-foot-long, hardwood logs. After we had hammered the spore-plugs into the holes, we took the logs to the back of the cabin where dad dropped them into an old bathtub filled with water. He weighted them with some cement blocks to soak for a day or two then stood them up against the back of the cabin in the moist shade to germinate. I don't remember how long it was before he had mushrooms, but the end product was both dramatic and delicious. He freeze-dried his harvest and kept the mushrooms in shrink-wrapped bags. The only visual evidence I have of dad's mushroom production is a woodcarving I gave him for Christmas in 1995.

I have a special fondness for mushrooms. They are elegant and beautiful, but they can also look like dog vomit. They are delicious, but they might kill you. As the saying goes, all mushrooms are edible, but some of them only once.

38

If I Could Talk to the Animals...

Published December 2, 2021

I usually enjoy the animal sounds in my backyard, but this squirrel was getting on my last nerve. I was reading on my back porch enjoying a balmy, fall afternoon. He was sitting on top of the gate arbor twenty feet away squawking at me—or so it seemed.

He was making that peculiar squirrel sound, "chirl, chirl, chirl," over and over and over.

I try to stay attuned to all those chirps, twitters, and squawks when creatures talk to each other. It is as though they are speaking in a foreign language. I am sure they mean something. I just don't understand what it is. Most of the sounds are pleasant and melodic. Some sounds—like that squirrel—can be annoying. But I recently heard an animal sound that was other-worldly.

If I had been walking in the woods in a dense fog, I would have thought this was the musical score of a sci-fi movie and a flying saucer had just landed. But this music was all too real. I was outdoors on an early June evening in Louisville, Kentucky and the buzzing, musical sound was the height of the seventeen-year cicada emergence. The noise at times was deafening.

Every seventeen years, billions of cicadas from what is known as Brood X tunnel up from underground to spend their final days trying to attract a mate. The cicadas I was listening to began their lives in 2004, when newly hatched nymphs fell from the trees, burrowed into the dirt, and fed on sap from the rootlets of grasses and trees as they slowly matured. All that preparation had been leading up to the moment when they surface in droves—up to 1.4 million cicadas per acre—to molt into their adult form, sing their deafening love song, and produce the next generation before dying just a few weeks later.

The sound of an individual cicada sounds like the rapid clicking of an old-fashioned telegraph machine. It is actually just the love song of males trying to attract a mate, but when they all sing together it is said to be the loudest animal sound on the planet.

At the other end of the spectrum is the animal song I heard on a cool overcast afternoon in July 1997. I had just boarded a small boat with a half-dozen other people for a whale-watching cruise. This was not one of those large-scale ocean cruises, because these whales were spending the summer in an estuary at the mouth of northern Canada's Churchill River. As our small boat motored away from the dock into Hudson Bay, I was skeptical about seeing whales. The water was calm, but the river was wide at this point and very murky. How we were to find whales, I had no idea, but as it turned out, we did not need to find them. They found us.

About twenty minutes into our cruise, they just appeared around the boat. There was no way to count them because they bobbed up to blow and breathe, then sank back down. I suppose there were ten or fifteen animals—many of them longer than our boat.

When the guide on our excursion lowered a microphone, called a hydrophone, into the water, we heard the high-pitched chirps, squeaks, and squeals of wild beluga whales coming from the small boom box at the back of the boat. It was the chatter of a whale family on an outing, talking to each other as they made their way up the river. They seemed unconcerned over our presence—innocent and vulnerable.

The beluga whale (*Delphinapterus leucas*) is an Arctic and sub-Arctic cetacean. It has unique characteristics that are adapted to life in the Arctic. These include its all-white color and the absence of a dorsal fin, which allows belugas to swim under the ice. The beluga's body size is between that of a dolphin and a true whale, with males growing up to eighteen feet long and weighing over three thousand pounds.

Belugas are gregarious and form groups of a dozen-or-so animals, although during the summer, they can gather in the hundreds or even thousands in estuaries and shallow coastal areas. Belugas depend heavily on underwater sound for orientation, feeding, and communication. They use echolocation for movement, to find breathing holes in the ice, and to hunt in dark or turbid waters. In addition to the clicks they use for navigation, these animals communicate using sounds of high-frequency whistles. Their calls can sound like bird songs, earning them the nickname "canaries of the sea."

There is heavy debate as to whether cetacean vocalizations can constitute a language. A study conducted in 2015 determined that European beluga signals share physical features comparable to "vowels." These sounds were found to be stable throughout time but varied among different geographical locations. Like most true languages, the further away the populations were from each other, the more varied the sounds were in relation to one another.

Hearing the belugas, cicadas, and squirrels reminded me of Carl Sagan's 1985 science fiction novel, *Contact*. It deals with the exciting prospect of human contact with intelligent, extraterrestrial life. It is almost amusing to think about humans trying to communicate with an intelligent, extraterrestrial life-form when we can't—or won't—communicate with each other. We are divided by language, by politics, and by, well, bull-headed stubbornness.

We clearly have much to learn about communication. One way I have attempted to improve my own communication skill is to listen more closely to the chirps, caws, and melodies of the animals in my own backyard. But I still don't know what that squirrel was worried about. I was just sitting there on my porch. Surely, he wasn't worried about me. Finally, I got up to see what the fuss was about. Maybe there was a cat lurking in the shrubbery below the porch. Or maybe a snake was slithering up the crepe myrtle in his direction. But on closer inspection, I still couldn't see any threat. As I eased in his direction, he turned and scampered down the fence.

I'm not sure but I think he cast a look back at me with a sly smile on his thin, squirrelly lips. I wonder if he won a bet with his friends back up the tree. He got me up, out of my chair, and outside to investigate… nothing. I took a moment to "communicate" what I thought of him and went back inside to continue my reading.

39

Beginning the Slow Process of Saying Farewell

Published December 22, 2021

Not many people get to retire twice, but I did when I said goodbye to my mules, Mike and Ike. My days on the wagon watching quail hunters stalk the South Georgia pine forest had come to an end as I prepared for big changes in the new year.

In fact, my changes began with Christmas of that year because for the first time in forty years, we wouldn't be loading the car with gifts and driving to Louisville, Kentucky. The years of celebrating the season in my wife's childhood home on Tyler Lane ended when her father died earlier that year. Elmer Liebert was the last of our parents and the sale of his house meant life-long traditions had passed. We would need to find new ways to celebrate Christmas.

When you get to retirement age, big life changes aren't necessarily a good thing. Our elderly parents have passed away and suddenly my wife and I are the oldest generation in the family. Gone are the days of exciting promotions and pay raises at work, sitting in bleachers at our children's sporting events, or learning a new skill. A good day is when I can go for a walk and not need a handful of ibuprofen when I get home. A triumph is remembering why I walked into a room to get something. And sleeping through the night without having to get up two or three times to stumble to the bathroom is, well, unheard of.

So, when we bought a house in Atlanta, I began to feel like a kid again. We wouldn't move until Karen retired at the end of the school year, but the honey-do list for the new house grew by the day. And with the excitement of the move came the months of anticipation and the endless goodbyes. At some point, I would take my final walk around the neighborhood, say goodbye to my Sunday School class, and walk out of Calhoun State Prison with my Kairos volunteer ministry team for the last time. Karen was already facing her school year of "finals"—the final first day of school, the final book fair, and the final Christmas break.

There would be plenty for us to miss about life in Albany. I would miss all the retired Marines in their red pickup trucks with Semper Fi stickers. I would miss Pretoria Fields Brown Thrasher Ale, the Festival of Lights at Chehaw, the five-minute drives to Publix and Home Depot. But all my life, I have made the most unlikely of moves. As a young zookeeper who grew up on the sandy beaches of Florida, I moved to Canada in the fall of 1973 to face my first Arctic winter at the Toronto Zoo. Karen and I moved from Louisville to Tampa to Sioux Falls to Toledo to Greenville, South Carolina before settling in Albany seventeen years ago. Now, in retirement, we have once again taken the unconventional route. We did not retire to a cabin in the mountains or a beachside bungalow. We relocated to the heart of one of the biggest cities in America.

Our new home in Atlanta is within walking distance of four microbreweries and a pub called the Stratford, which has trivia night on Wednesdays. We have a neighborhood with sidewalks, a home with a basement, and an elementary school across the street. We'll enjoy the Christmas lights at the Atlanta Botanical Garden, the Atlanta Opera's performance of the *Pirates of Penzance*, and summer Braves games at Truist Park. And while my fellow Atlantans are stuck in traffic on their way to and from work, I'll be perched at my new writing desk looking out on my new backyard where Karen will be constructing her new garden.

I will, of course, need to find a new outlet for my writing. *Albany Herald* readers probably won't want to hear about my new life in that big city to the north. And the big city newspapers won't be interested in the musings of a small-town writer. Since I retired in 2016, I've written about sixty articles for the *Albany Herald*. I've covered mules and dogs, nature and COVID, Albany history, and my own personal life. Maybe there is another book in all of that.

One of the oddest experiences so far occurred on the day I resigned from driving the wagon. As I drove home from the plantation, I reflected on my experiences and the many people whose lives crossed mine. But the greatest sadness came from an unexpected source. I never said goodbye to the ones I came to admire most. I was in direct contact with them for countless hours over the last few years. I learned from them and came to love being around them. I'll cherish the time I spent with my mules, Mike and Ike, as much as anything else in recent memory.

I can't say their feelings toward me are mutual, but I do recall the time a couple of months ago when I was loading them into the horse trailer, and I slipped and fell. As I lay flat on my back looking up at two, half-ton mules with hooves as big as dinner plates, I thought I might be a goner. But they both stood unnaturally still. I grabbed a harness, pulled myself to my feet and stumbled outside to catch my breath. Working with those mules touched my spirit in ways I didn't expect.

So, in spite of the adage, "You can't teach an old dog new tricks," this old dog is looking forward to a new year, a new home, and some new adventures.

40

The Southern Plantation

Published January 19, 2022

I don't consider myself particularly "woke" in the modern vernacular, but I did find myself uncomfortable admitting in my books that I drove a mule wagon on a southern "plantation." The term seems widely accepted in the South, but my books are read in other parts of the world. That is why I self-consciously referred to my employer as a hunting "lodge." In an era when the master bedroom is now called the primary or main bedroom, how is it that we have large tracts of southern property that we still call plantations?

To be fair, the plantation that employed me on Gillionville Road outside Albany, Georgia was established long after slavery was abolished. From the time it was purchased in the late 1800s until it ceased operation and was sold in 2019, Gillionville Plantation had been devoted to hunting—especially bobwhite quail.

Plantation comes from the Latin word *plantare*, meaning "to plant." Oxford Reference broadens it to "an estate on which crops such as coffee, sugar, and tobacco are grown, especially in former colonies and once worked by slaves." A plantation, then, is actually just a place where crops are grown. But it is that last bit that makes it such a highly charged term, and for good reason.

So, I did a little research. Modern plantations weren't built on the backs of slaves, and they aren't preserved like monuments to Civil War generals. Many modern plantations are historic sites that educate visitors about the horrors of slavery. Others have been turned into wildlife habitat and forestry preserves, harkening back to their original meaning as estates on which crops are grown.

Plantations have been around since the ancient Romans developed large farms called *latifundia*, which used slave or paid labor to grow crops and livestock for sale. New World plantations began in the mid-1600s when slave traders brought workers for the sugar and coffee plantations of the West Indies. During the American Colonial period, plantations existed as far north as the Hudson River valley of New York, but this type of agriculture eventually became synonymous with the South. During the early seventeenth century, English colonists in the southern part of North America began looking for ways to produce goods or raise crops that could be sold for a profit in England or Europe. Colonists experimented with raising mulberry trees to support silkworms for making silk. They also tried growing grapes for wine production and harvesting trees for timber. But it was the indigenous American tobacco plant that emerged as the crop that offered the greatest potential for profitability. Tobacco, however, required hundreds of acres of land, it quickly drained the soil of nutrients, and it needed a large labor force to tend the fields and to harvest and prepare the crop for market.

At first, colonists used indentured servants, who worked up to seven years without pay in exchange for their passage to the English colonies. But by the eighteenth century, owners of large plantations found it more profitable to purchase African slaves, who they could own and who would provide free labor for their lifetime. As Europeans began settling in the Carolinas and Georgia in the late seventeenth and early eighteenth centuries, they began experimenting with raising rice, indigo (used in making dye), and cotton for the market, all of which also required extensive acreage and free labor. Thus, the first two centuries of European settlement in the southern part of North America firmly established a new definition of a plantation: a very large farm that used slave labor to produce a commodity for export.

The plantation model was so widely accepted that early presidents were slave-owning plantation owners. George Washington's Mount Vernon and Thomas Jefferson's Monticello are the best-known examples. But consider Ambrose Madison, a planter and slaveholder in Virginia, who arrived in 1732 at a plantation he called, ironically for the slaves who built it, Mount Pleasant. One of Ambrose's grandchildren, James, spent his early childhood at Mount Pleasant while construction began on a brick Georgian house that would later become the center of President James Madison's Montpelier.

And there was Andrew Jackson's Hermitage Plantation near Nashville, Tennessee. It was a self-sustaining property that relied on slave labor to produce cotton. When he first bought The Hermitage in 1804, Jackson owned nine African slaves. At the time of his death forty years later, about 150 slaves lived and worked on the property.

Plantations were common in all the states of the upper south from Virginia to Louisiana and northern Florida to Kentucky.

The oldest of Georgia's tidewater estates, Wormsloe Plantation in Savannah, was developed by Noble Jones who came to Georgia with James Oglethorpe in 1733. In fact, many of Georgia's earliest plantations began around Savannah in the 1700s. Mulberry Grove Plantation in Chatham County twelve miles northwest of Savannah, for example, was an active plantation from 1736 until the end of the Civil War when the great plantation house was destroyed by General Sherman during his march to the sea. The significance of Mulberry Grove included support for Georgia's silk industry with its large mulberry nursery. When the silk industry failed, it turned its low marsh acreage to rice and became one of the leading rice plantations along the Savannah River. And Mulberry Grove is also famous as the place where Eli Whitney developed the cotton gin in 1793.

Owing to the size of the state and its being the southernmost of the original colonies, Georgia has an extensive list of nearly three dozen early plantations that still exist. Many of them operate as historic sites that include reenactors and historic tours. The Jarrell Plantation State Historic Site, for example, is a state park on a former cotton plantation in Juliette, Georgia. Located in the red clay hills of the Georgia piedmont north of Macon, the site stands as one of the best-preserved examples of a "middle class" southern plantation.

According to the Library of Congress, the importation of captives for enslavement was provided for in the U.S. Constitution and continued to take place on a large scale even after it was made illegal in 1808. The slave system was one of the principal engines of the new nation's financial independence, and it grew steadily until it was abolished by war. In 1790 there were fewer than 700,000 enslaved people in the United States. By 1830, there were more than two million and on the eve of the Civil War, nearly four million were enslaved—with nearly a half-million of them living in Georgia.

When slavery ended in 1865, another form of labor replaced it. Many freed African Americans had no choice but to return to the plantations to work as sharecroppers or as tenant farmers who rented land from white owners. Both tenant farmers and sharecroppers raised cotton, livestock, and other agricultural products that primarily benefited the white plantation owners. But with the end of free slave labor, the old profitability model of the plantation became unsustainable. By the late 1800s, plantations were failing and falling into disrepair. That is when wealthy Northerners began buying up property at bargain-basement prices and resurrecting those plantations using a very different model.

Dozens of properties that call themselves plantations still dot the landscape in southwest Georgia between Albany and Thomasville. Gillionville Plantation, where I drove the mule-wagon, was one of them. It may have once been a cotton plantation, but it was transformed into acreage that was befitting the original meaning of the word plantation.

By the time I climbed on the wagon in 2016, South Georgia had become world-famous as a quail hunting destination. Plantations were synonymous with quail hunting and were actively developing and preserving thousands of acres of the signature, natural ecosystem of the American southeast—the longleaf pine savanna. But how these properties went from cotton fields to prime quail habitat is another story.

41

The Fire Bird

Published February 2, 2022

I grew up thinking fire was the enemy of the forest. It killed trees, injured animals, and spawned a ruined, blackened landscape. I saw the horrors of a forest fire as a child when I watched the Walt Disney classic, *Bambi*. It wasn't until I took over management of Chehaw Park in Albany, Georgia that I learned the truth about the benefits of fire from our Natural Resources Manager, Ben Kirkland.

I assumed it was Smokey Bear and the U.S. Forest Service that had steered me wrong with the admonition "Only YOU can prevent forest fires!" But in truth, the problem was much older than Smokey Bear—who came on the scene in the 1940s—and it was plantation owners who shattered a dangerous myth and helped save the southern forests.

In the early 1920s, plantation owners around Thomasville, Georgia noticed a serious decline in quail populations and feared that the birds might become extinct in the region. They recognized the need for a scientific study of the bobwhite (*Colinus virginianus*) in hopes of reversing the decline. So, in the fall of 1922 they reached out to Herbert L. Stoddard, a thirty-three-year-old naturalist, ornithologist, and taxidermist who ran the bird department at the Milwaukee Public Museum.

To finance the quail research project, plantation owners organized. They dug into their own pockets, reached out to friends, and raised the necessary funds. By fall 1923, Stoddard was stalking the woods between

Thomasville and Tallahassee trapping quail, studying what they ate, and what ate them. He had no college degree—no formal education or scientific training. But, as it turned out, that is what allowed him to discover the real problem that faced the bobwhite quail and the habitat they needed to survive.

Stoddard was from the North but had spent much of his boyhood in central Florida. He was well familiar with the practice of Florida cattlemen and Native Americans who intentionally set fire to their land. One of his first recommendations was that the effects of burning might be important to the Thomasville quail studies.

"The bobwhite," Stoddard noted in his 1969 book, *Memoirs of a Naturalist*, "might properly be called the 'fire bird' so closely is it linked ecologically with fire in the coastal pinelands."

He knew that quail thrive in the aftermath of fire. He told the plantation owners that quail need the perennial legumes and grasses that sprout after fire. Excluding fire allowed the buildup of what he called "rough" habitat. The thick cover of shrubs and small hardwood trees favored rodents—especially cotton rats—which attracted predators like foxes, birds of prey, and the huge abundant diamondback rattlesnakes he encountered when he first moved to Georgia. It was exactly the wrong habitat for bobwhite quail. His clients apparently bought his argument. Others were skeptical at best. Some were downright hostile.

Stoddard was classified by the professional forestry community as an enemy of the forests because he not only suggested southern forests *could* be burned but insisted they *should* be burned. He introduced the concept of "controlled burning" or "prescribed fire" to maintain natural vegetation and wildlife.

In those days U.S. Forest Service was against any use of fire for land management purposes, even in in the southeast where fire was a natural process. American forestry, Stoddard noted, was rooted in European (especially German) forestry practices where there were no fire-type forests. In addition, all U.S. forestry schools in those days were located in the North where forestry classes and textbooks did not acknowledge fire-type forests. Forestry experts assumed fire would have a disastrous effect on game and wildlife management. They pointed to uncontrolled wildfires in the western mountains and in the northern forests. At the American Forestry Association meeting in February 1929, Stoddard presented the chapter on fire from his soon-to-be-published book *The Bobwhite Quail: Its Habits, Preservation, and Increase* to the assembly. He was greeted, he recalled, with "great hostility."

The Forest Service eventually came around and today burning the southern pine forests is accepted practice. The Georgia Forestry Commission and the Georgia Prescribed Fire Council say prescribed fire "is a safe way to apply a natural process, ensure ecosystem health and reduce wildfire risks." They note that habitats across the state have evolved with fire and that the strategic application of fire mimics this natural cycle. Even Smokey Bear has updated his message to "Only You Can Prevent *Wildfires*" in an attempt to clarify that he is promoting the prevention of unplanned outdoor fires, not prescribed burns.

At most modern plantations, prescribed fire is the primary land management tool for thousands of acres of forest and wildlife resources. At Robert W. Woodruff's Ichauway Plantation, for example, I saw fire used on a massive scale during my first visit there in the fall of 2004. According to the website of the Jones Center at Ichauway, healthy longleaf pine forests depend on frequent fire. In the absence of fire, longleaf pine forests shift to hardwood dominated forests over time. The unique plants and animals found in longleaf pine forests have adapted to frequent fire and depend on it to maintain their preferred habitat structure.

The pine forests of the southeastern United States are thought to have once covered fifty percent of the land across thousands of miles of nine states from Virginia to Texas. The late biologist E. O. Wilson once identified twelve of the best places on earth to see a living natural environment. He placed our longleaf pine savanna in the same category as the Amazon rainforest and the Serengeti grasslands.

A hundred years ago, plantation owners brought in a maverick, Yankee forester who convinced them to go against all the "experts" and burn their property. They bought his radical concept, and they are still burning today. Without the stewardship of these wealthy landlords and the radical ideas of Herbert Stoddard, southwest Georgia probably wouldn't have thousands of acres of one of the world's most important natural ecosystems—the southern pine forest.

42

The Tortoise and the Billionaire

Published February 9, 2022

It was one of those moments that passes almost without a thought. We've all done it a thousand times. Like when we are driving along in our car and suddenly, we arrive at our destination without any recollection of how we got there. For me, it happened on the first quail hunt of the season with my employer and his family and friends. The mules were behaving nicely on this splendid, warm October morning, so I was driving the wagon along the trail watching where I was going but allowing my mind to wander.

The two-thousand-acre property where we were hunting is a few miles northeast of Tallahassee, Florida. It was once called Chemonie Plantation. Its history is said to date back to the early 1800s after President Andrew Jackson forced out the Seminole Indians. Chemonie began as a slave-holding plantation that grew cotton, corn, and sugarcane. It succeeded until the Civil War freed the enslaved people it relied on for that success. When the owners went bust, the fields turned back into their natural scrub.

This is when the second wave of owners swept into South Georgia and North Florida around the turn of the twentieth century. America was in the midst of the Industrial Revolution so oil barons, automobile dealers, and company CEOs had plenty of disposable income. They were drawn to the huge population of quail in the grasslands of these plantations.

They bought property and turned it into prime hunting lands that soon became highly sought after by bird hunters worldwide. Chemonie has been sold and divided several times and now operates under another name. The current owners of the property are remarkably similar to the people who first started the post-war hunting plantations nearly 150 years ago. They enjoy being outdoors. They love hunting quail. And they are happy to put their considerable resources to work preserving quail habitat. It is where my wagon driving career continued after Gillionville Plantation in Albany, Georgia ceased operation, and where I finally retired from wagon driving at the end of 2021.

One of the challenges of driving a mule wagon through the woods is "road hazards" like logs, stumps, and gopher holes. They can wreck an expensive, custom-built wagon and ruin a hunt. As I bounced along the path deep in thought I guided the mules to the right with a gentle tug on the reins. I had noticed a gopher tortoise burrow at the edge of the road. It was unmistakable—its flat floor and domed arch perfectly matching the shell of what must have been a large tortoise. The yellow sand that had been excavated out of the hole was spread halfway across the cart-path.

As we rumbled along, it took me a few minutes to register what I had just witnessed. Nobody on my wagon commented on the obvious sign of gopher tortoise activity and the six people on horseback ahead of me took no notice either. If it had been a deer, a turkey, or even a hog they would have been excited. I was the only person who was pleased to see signs of a tortoise and was left to wonder how many other tortoise burrows were spread around this property.

Two thousand acres is a lot of space and I spent most of my wagon-driving days lost in its vastness. There were few signs of the civilization that surrounded us. It was home to countless critters, but the gopher tortoise is special. It was designated Georgia's state reptile in 1989 and is now listed as "threatened." That is why I was silently disappointed that nobody—including the owners of the property—took notice.

The family I worked for as a wagon driver fit the twenty-first–century profile of the quail hunting pioneers. I don't talk about my employers out of respect for their privacy, but their story and contribution to conservation is too important to ignore. Most quail hunting properties utilize jeeps and ATVs to move hunters around. It takes deep pockets to hunt with horses, mules, and wagons. My employers wanted an experience that was closer to the land. They hired talented people, built quality facilities for the dogs and hoofed stock, and purchased expensive wagons to haul supplies for the hunt. They also reintroduced controlled burning to the property.

If my employers had wanted to add to their already considerable wealth, they might have been better served to develop the property. We were fifteen minutes from I-10, a few miles from downtown Tallahassee. It was prime real estate and much of the surrounding area had already been turned into subdivisions and commercial property. I had seen the process unfold in the woods around my boyhood home in St. Petersburg, Florida.

I didn't know it at the time, but the Florida woods where I grew up is called pine flatwoods and it is said to represent the most extensive type of terrestrial ecosystem in Florida. Approximately fifty percent of Central Florida's natural land area is pine flatwoods—forests that are dominated by southern slash pine and interspersed with an understory of saw palmetto and mixed grasses. But the acres of pine flatwoods where my brothers and I roamed as boys were gradually swallowed up in development until they became one giant subdivision of housing. The deer, fox squirrels, rabbits, tortoises, and quail disappeared.

This is what struck me as we trundled past this lone gopher tortoise burrow on a pleasant October morning—the image of my childhood woods now being covered by a subdivision. Even though the owners of this property can ride past an obvious tortoise burrow without noticing, they are preserving that tortoise without realizing it. I don't mind that the property is owned by rich people who love to shoot birds. I also don't care that it is private property and not a park that is open to the public. It may even be better for the animals this way.

Just before lunchtime, I came to understand just how fortunate the animals on this land were. We had just come up a rise and crested a hill. There spread out before us was a large lake nestled in the rolling hills. Its blue waters sparkled in the late morning sun and a bald eagle soared overhead.

We had been passing through beautiful countryside all morning and I had been listening to the conversations on my wagon. I knew what one of my passengers was going to say, because I saw it myself. As we glided to a stop to honor the dogs on-point, the man stood up from his seat behind me, pointed to the lake, and exclaimed to his seatmate, "My God, this would make a beautiful golf hole."

Plantations have been preserving irreplaceable wildlife habitat for more than a hundred years and I hope they will continue their stewardship. Thank goodness my employers were hunters and not golfers or property developers!

43

Ready to Live a Life in the Fast Lane

Published March 24, 2022

People in South Georgia gave me the side-eye when I told them I was moving to Atlanta.

"The traffic up there is terrible," they somberly informed me with an *are-you-out-of-your-mind* kind of look.

"Oh, really!" the bubble of sarcasm above my head said, "I hadn't noticed."

What I actually said is, "I know that, but since I will be retired, I don't much care."

When I drove the mule-drawn wagon on a quail hunting plantation, I was reminded of the slow pace of the lives of our ancestors. I wondered what it would be like for me to drive to work every morning on my wagon. I wouldn't need to worry about traffic jams or speed traps.

My mules pulled an old-fashioned wagon with a heavy wooden body and tall, spoked (albeit rubber-tired) wheels. It was not a stretch to imagine a time when this type of transportation was the norm. My 200-mile, three-hour drive to Atlanta, according to Google maps, would take more than two days on a wagon. Imagine needing to stop at a Motel 6 halfway to Atlanta!

At the end of every hunt, we had a fifteen- or twenty-minute ride back to the house. The pointers were back in the wagon and the retriever was lying on the seat beside me as I followed the horse riders. The only sound was the jingle of the mule harnesses, the conversation of the guests, and the occasional bobwhite quail whistling in the tall grass. The pace was slow enough for a person to walk but I never heard a guest complain about the length of our ride. In fact, people often remarked on how peaceful it was and how they could feel their blood pressure going down—a sensation that is unlikely when we travel today.

We drive to Atlanta twice a month to work on the new house. It is a pleasant drive up Highway 280 to Columbus where we get on I-185 then I-85 and on to Atlanta. It is usually smooth sailing until we get near our destination, because the closer we get to Atlanta the faster people drive. We are bumper to bumper by the time we get on the I-285 beltway, and I struggle to keep up with the dense traffic. Even going more than 70 MPH, cars pass me like I am standing still. They cut across multiple lanes of traffic, weave between speeding cars and trucks, and dart in front of me to get to the nearest exit. On my last trip, I saw a car drive along the right-hand emergency pull-off lane to pass multiple cars who weren't going fast enough. What, I wonder, is the hurry?

There are only two things that might make a driver slow down. One is when eight lanes of traffic come to a complete stop. The other I see on those rare occasions when I am going fast enough to pass someone. Invariably they are not watching the road. They have one hand on the wheel and their eyes glued to a cell phone as they drift from lane to lane.

Now, I like to drive fast. That is why I usually set my cruise control when I am on the open road. Otherwise, I will find myself driving over the speed limit when I round the bend and see that highway patrol vehicle parked in the median. But there is no cruise control on the Atlanta freeways. You are either going way too slow in the middle lane or thrust into the slipstream of cars and trucks with your hands at ten and two on the steering wheel, your speedometer in the mid-80s, and your heart thumping in your chest.

And then there are the fools who drive too fast for conditions. One recent Sunday morning, I was on the Stone Mountain Freeway on my way to have a tire repaired. It was raining and I was driving on the spare tire. I struggled along at 55 MPH so, as usual, cars were passing me right and left. Suddenly there was a white work van passing me on my left—but it was traveling backward. I did a double take as the van slowed down and faded from view. I glanced in my rearview mirror. Somebody must have hydroplaned because cars were spinning out on the rain-slick road behind me. A car veered into the median and another careened off the road to the right as the white van came to a stop in the middle of the highway.

As I viewed the chaos behind me, I slowed a little and relaxed in my seat. For the moment I was alone on the road, so I turned up the radio and recalled my time on the wagon when the mules were in harness, a dog rested on my lap, and life was moving at a peaceful pace. In the blink of an eye, I had gone from adrenaline-fueled stress on the roadway to absolute calm. Welcome to life in the big city.

44

Horace King, the Bridge Builder

Published February 16 and 24, 2022

As a white child of the Jim Crow South, I probably have little right to opine on black greatness. But during Black History Month, I keep thinking about someone I have admired since I learned his story when I moved to Albany, Georgia. He is seldom mentioned in the same breath as the likes of Rosa Parks or Martin Luther King. But he and I are kindred spirits even though he was black, and we were born nearly 150 years apart.

We both became Masons when we lived in Ohio—he in Oberlin and me a few miles to the west in Toledo. We both love to build things—I build furniture and he built bridges. And we both love our mules. He once sued the federal government to try to recover some mules the Union Army "requisitioned" from him during the Civil War.

According to the Alabama Heritage website of the University of Alabama, Horace King was born in South Carolina on September 8, 1807. Little is known of his early life, but he appears to have acquired considerable knowledge and skill as a master carpenter and bridge builder. He was a type of slave known as a craftsman.

Craftsman slaves had learned highly sought-after skills. They were carpenters, blacksmiths, and teamsters and they were often hired out by their owners to make money. Usually, their earnings went to the master, but some craftsmen were allowed to keep some of their money and perhaps even work unsupervised. A few even set their own wages and arrange their own jobs. Horace King became one of these.

He was purchased when in his early twenties by John Godwin, the son of a prominent South Carolina businessman. Godwin was a builder who learned the bridge-building innovations of Connecticut architect Ithiel Town. Town's design, which he had patented in 1820, was called the "Town Lattice Truss." It was an entirely new system of wooden framework that could be erected using inexpensive common sawmill lumber and the labor of any carpenter's gang.

The system used upright, two-by-ten, rough-cut planks along the walls of the bridge that were set at an angle in a crisscross pattern. The boards were fastened where they crossed with a couple of two-inch diameter, wooden pegs called "tree nails." This allowed a span of a little over a hundred feet before the structure needed support from below, usually in the form of a stone tower or pier. A roof added structure to the bridge and protected the wooden framework from rot. Much of the assembly occurred in a field nearby where the wall boards could be fastened together while flat on the ground. The wall sections were then transported to the job site and erected—an early example of prefab construction.

It is likely that John Godwin and Horace King, became acquainted with Town's innovative truss design at a construction site in South Carolina because both Godwin and King were familiar with the Town Lattice Truss before they left South Carolina for Columbus, Georgia in 1832.

John Godwin, doing business as "John Godwin, Bridge Builder," had submitted a bid to construct the first public bridge over the Chattahoochee River. His bid was accepted, and Godwin and King began work in May 1832. In July they advertised in the Columbus Enquirer for stone masons to work on the piers of the bridge and by August the project was well underway. When completed in 1833, the 900-foot-long covered bridge earned Godwin and King reputations as master bridge builders and work began to flow their way.

Apparently, from the beginning of their relationship, Horace King was treated more as a junior partner in Godwin's company than a slave. Godwin developed proposals and King supervised construction. In addition to building bridges, King spent much of the 1830s and 1840s working on the buildings and houses that the Godwin firm built around Columbus and Girard (now Phenix City), Alabama, where they had taken up residence. King's ability to supervise massive construction projects and to elicit superior workmanship from mixed gangs of laborers, both slave and free, impressed some of the most successful businessmen in the South.

One of these men was Robert Jemison, Jr., of Tuscaloosa, Alabama. Jemison was a lawyer and state senator who owned a large and well-organized network of interrelated businesses that included a stagecoach line, a turnpike and bridge company, and extensive sawmill operations. In the early 1840s, Jemison began contracting with Godwin for bridges in Alabama. Horace King supervised the construction. After several joint ventures with Godwin and King, Jemison wrote a testimonial to Godwin in 1845 that praised King's "style and dispatch" and "the impressive manner in which [King] has conducted himself."

As King's fortunes rose, however, those of his master declined. By 1846 Godwin had suffered a series of financial setbacks. Realizing that King could be taken from him to settle debts with his creditors, Godwin arranged with Robert Jemison to petition the Alabama General Assembly for King's release from slavery. After Godwin posted the required $1,000 bond Jemison succeeded, and on February 3, 1846, Horace King became a free man.

A few years later, King was contracted to build a bridge across the Oconee River in Milledgeville, Georgia. He set up his prefab operation and began the project, but a disagreement arose over payment for the bridge. When King and his employers were unable to come to terms, what happened next seems extraordinary to me and is, perhaps, an indication of King's character and resolve.

Horace King, a black man doing business in the pre-Civil War South, walked out on his white employers. He loaded the timbers, lattices, and other bridge materials onto railroad flatcars and moved them to another project. An enterprising south Georgia businessman had heard all about Horace King and was anxious to acquire his services. The man was Nelson Tift, who wanted to build a bridge across the Flint River in Albany, Georgia.

I can't imagine a more unlikely pair of business partners. Horace King, the hard-headed former slave who walked out on his last project because of business differences and Nelson Tift, the hard-driving businessman who was, according to the New Georgia Encyclopedia, "committed wholly to slave society." King was probably still irritated at white people trying to take advantage of him on his last job. Tift was a slave owner who also came to the Albany bridge project with a thorn in his side. He was paying for the bridge out of his own pocket after he had failed to interest either the city or the county in the idea. (Oh, to be a fly on the wall at their first meeting!)

Born in 1810 to a Connecticut mercantile family, Nelson Tift followed his father into business and headed south. He moved around for a few years before he settled in Albany, Georgia in October 1836. Tift's business acumen saw him speculating in land, operating a dry goods store and several mills, and acquiring the rights to operate a ferry and, later, a toll bridge across the Flint River.

It is worth noting that, even though he used the services of Horace King, a freed slave, Tift was deeply committed to the principles of slavery. He owned slaves himself and as a member of the Georgia legislature, he supported the reopening of the international slave trade (which had been prohibited by law since 1808) as a way to encourage ownership of enslaved people to all white Georgians. He died a wealthy man in 1891.

Little is apparently known about Horace King's bridge across the Flint River, except that it was completed in 1858. Judging by the location of the Bridge House and its corresponding bank across the river, it must have been at least 300 feet across. A comparable bridge can be seen at Watson Mill Bridge State Park near Comer, Georgia. Watson Mill Bridge claims to be the longest covered bridge in the state, spanning 229 feet across. It was built in 1885, the year of King's death, by Horace King's oldest son, Washington. He, of course, used Ithiel Town's Lattice Truss and tree-nail system. At one time, according to the Georgia State Parks website, Georgia had more than two-hundred covered bridges but today, fewer than twenty remain. Most of them gave way to fire, flood, or the ravages of time on untreated wood.

After he left Albany, Horace King spent the rest of his long life as a prosperous builder and businessman. He died on May 28, 1885, at the age of seventy-eight, but his legacy goes far beyond his buildings. When his former owner, John Godwin died in 1859, his estate was insolvent. As a testimony to how much the Godwin children honored Horace King, they formally recorded in the Russell County Courthouse that "Horace King is duly emancipated and freed from all claims held by us." They knew that as a former slave, King could be held accountable for their father's debts.

King remained close to the Godwin family, helping Godwin's son run the failing family business. In addition, King quietly provided for his former master's family. According to one of King's contemporaries, Godwin's children "became [King's] wards at his own option."

But perhaps the most telling legacy of Horace King is a monument he purchased and erected on the grave of his former master. The inscription reads:

John Godwin Born Oct. 17, 1798. Died Feb. 26, 1859. This stone was placed here by Horace King, in lasting remembrance of the love and gratitude he felt for his lost friend and former master.

The monument bears the Masonic emblem, the square and compasses, which marks Godwin as a Mason. In fact, the monument is presented from one Mason to another.

Faye Gibbons notes in her 2002 book, *Horace King, Bridges to Freedom*, that two years after Godwin's death, King was in Ohio visiting friends and seeking to join the Masons—something that was not allowed for a black man in the South. After he became a Mason, King obviously took to heart its principles of brotherly love, relief, and truth and he would have been especially concerned about the Masonic care of widows and orphans—even those of his former slave master.

I am fascinated by the character and resolve of this former slave, turned craftsman, turned business owner. Following the Civil War, King served two terms in the Alabama legislature. He brought all five of his children—four sons and one daughter—into the business and formed the King Brothers Bridge Company. They went on to build courthouses, mills, public buildings, and, of course, hundreds of bridges. All the while, King cared for and supported the children of the man who once owned him.

Today, we may remember Horace King as what his contemporary Robert Jemison, called "the best practicing bridge builder in the South."

But to remember King simply as a builder of bridges sells the man far short. His greatest achievement may have been simply in his humanity.

45

Being Part of the "Village"

Published May 19, 2022

You must be of a certain age for your name to appear on the 1950 census. My name made it—just barely. Sometime in April of 1950, a census enumerator named Mildred Poldemus knocked on the door at 2120 38th Avenue North in St. Petersburg, Florida. On her carefully handwritten form, she noted the residents: James M. Porter, a twenty-five-year-old plasterer; Carol, his twenty-year-old wife; and Lizzie, his sixty-six-year-old mother. Even though James was living in his mother's house, he—being a male—was listed as the head of the household. Also, in residence that day was James and Carol's five-month-old son whose name was listed as J. Douglas—yours truly. This is a bittersweet snapshot in time since I am the only person in that household still alive. Even the house is gone. It was demolished in the 1970s to make way for I-275.

Those 1950 Census records were released in April, exactly seventy-two years after enumerators like Mrs. Poldemus began knocking on doors. About forty-six million American houses were canvased and a little over 150 million people were counted. Those millions of census forms, painstakingly filled out by hand in ink, were just posted online by the National Archives and Records Administration, which by law has kept them private until now. Census records are confidential for seventy-two years to protect the privacy of the respondents.

The word census is Latin in origin. The Romans were counting their citizens by around the middle of the first millennium B.C. But few if any of those counts would meet today's definition, which is essentially to count everyone in a given place at a given time. The first census in the United States took place beginning on August 2, 1790. Although it took months to collect all the data from households.

During the 1950 census, according to the New York Times, the post-WWII baby boom was in full swing, the average family earned $3,300, and gasoline cost eighteen cents a gallon. About 140,000 census-takers, or enumerators, fanned out across the country that April. My father-in-law was one of them.

Elmer Liebert walked the Cherokee Park neighborhood in Louisville, Kentucky. He talked of going house to house, filling out his forms as he went. If nobody was home, he had to keep going back until they were available for interview. The 1950 census was the last complete house-to-house canvas. The next census in 1960 was conducted largely by mail. I know mail-in forms are much more efficient, but it seems a shame not to do a physical headcount.

A census form is more than a statistical headcount. It is as though someone has entered every home in America and taken a snapshot in time that tells a story. When Ms. Poldemus filled out that April 1950 census form, Carol Porter was just four months out of her teens. She was coming up on the first anniversary of her graduation from St. Pete High School. My dad was just beginning his career as a plasterer. They were struggling new parents who probably didn't know much about raising a child. They did such a good job with their four boys I always assumed it was down to their innate wisdom and superior parenting skills. But the census form suggests there may be more to it than that.

My mom always said she learned how to be a mother by living with her mother-in-law, Lizzie Porter. My Grandma Porter was born in November 1883. As a teenager she walked from Florida to Texas behind a covered wagon. She lived through two world wars and the Great Depression. She bore thirteen children and faced the burial of several of them. She told me, for example, that before the advent of baby food in jars, mothers would wean their children onto solid foods by chewing the food themselves before providing it to their babies. As a familiar insurance company television commercial says, Grandma Porter knew a thing or two because she'd seen a thing or two.

There is a widely quoted West African proverb, "It takes a village to raise a child." But my research indicates that the first appearance of the proverb in print may have been in a 1984 interview with author Toni Morrison who said, "it takes a village to raise a child, not one parent, not two parents, but the whole village."

As we celebrate our parents on Mother's Day and Father's Day, it might be useful to remember those who helped them along the way. I only saw my name on that census form because one of my sons was curious and searched the data the day after it came out. He started with his grandpa—my dad—and hit the jackpot. That same son, who lives in Kentucky, asked me to watch two of his children while he was on a business trip and my daughter-in-law was on a school trip with their middle son.

That's how this retired grandpa found himself in Louisville, Kentucky for a week playing—and losing—endless games of Clue with his nine-year-old grandson and seeing his seventeen-year-old granddaughter off on her first date. I'm not sure how much wisdom was passed along, but it felt right that I should be there. Those children have aunts and uncles, a church family, and other grandparents. But they also have this old man who sure enjoyed his time with them and is proud to be part of their "village."

46

Contemplating Tombstones and Our Burial Rituals

Published April 20, 2022

We had passed it on Interstate-85 before I realized what I had just seen. It was perched on a hill in the middle of the Exit-35 cloverleaf. Traffic was light on a Sunday afternoon and for a moment I thought about turning around to explore it. Who, I wondered, had placed it there and how in the world had someone engineered a highway on-ramp to avoid it? Then, as we drove on and my wife worked on her crossword puzzle, my mind really went to work. Why do we need cemeteries in the first place and why do we go to such extraordinary lengths to preserve them?

When my wife's father passed away, we buried him in Louisville, Kentucky's Cave Hill Cemetery next to Karen's mom. Elmer chose the site because it overlooked the property where he grew up. He had played on the cemetery grounds as a boy in the 1930s, and his father had even grazed Liebert Brothers Dairy cattle there before graves began expanding into that area of the property and a wall was erected.

Cave Hill Cemetery is a 300-acre, pre-Civil War era National Cemetery and arboretum. With its lush plantings, scenic lakes, and sweeping vistas, it is more like a public park than a place where the likes of Colonel Sanders and Muhammed Ali are interred.

The word *cemetery* comes from the Greek word for "sleeping place." It is a word that originally applied to places like the Roman catacombs and implies that the land is specifically designated as a burial ground. The term graveyard is often used interchangeably with cemetery, but a graveyard primarily refers to a burial ground within a churchyard.

The modern cemetery probably originated about a thousand years ago in Europe when burials were under the control of the church and could only take place on consecrated church ground. When churchyards began to fill up in the early 1800s, new locations were developed outside the population center. These early cemeteries were professionally designed, elaborately landscaped, and served as the first recreational areas in a time before public parks came into use.

Modern cemeteries offer a space that brings comfort to families as they struggle with their grief while remembering loved ones. They provide a serene environment in which to place flowers and remember the person who has passed.

All four of my grandparents are in Memorial Park Cemetery on 49th Street in St. Petersburg, Florida. I could visit their graves anytime and pause in remembrance. I visit my granddaughter's grave in Louisville whenever I am there. It is comforting to see her name etched in stone and remember her laughter and sweet disposition.

My parents, on the other hand, chose to be cremated. My brothers and I spread their ashes—half outside their cabin in the mountains of western North Carolina and half at the St. Petersburg beach that we frequented growing up. They have no headstones, monuments, or markers but for me, sitting in the sand at Pass-A-Grill Beach and reliving my childhood memories is at least as comforting as standing in a cemetery and looking at a granite marker.

I am not opposed to cemeteries, but I don't plan to have a headstone in one. My wife and I have talked about cremation rather than burial, but cremation seems a needless waste of fossil fuels. That is why we are also investigating more environmentally friendly options.

We could donate our bodies to science, an option that might contribute to the advancement of science and medicine. I wonder what name those med-students would give to my long, skinny cadaver. The name that comes to my mind is the tall, cadaverous Addams Family butler "Lurch"—a nickname that was hung on me in high school.

We briefly considered something called alkaline hydrolysis—a water-based dissolution process that uses heat, pressure, and alkali chemicals to gently break a human body down into chemical compounds. But as people who love nature and the outdoors, there are some even more attractive ways to become one with the earth.

We could be buried in something called a mushroom suit—a natural burial shroud made from biodegradable mushrooms and microorganisms. These organic materials aid in body decomposition and neutralize toxins, releasing nutrients into the surrounding environment and promoting new growth. Or we might consider human composting, a process that uses "organic reduction" to convert a human body into soil. It sounds almost too simple. The body is covered with natural materials such as straw and wood chips and left to decay. The resulting microbial activity breaks it down into clean, odorless soil that's free of pollutants and toxins. We have been composting organic material for our garden for years. I kind of like the idea that someone will haul my worn-out carcass to the backyard and let it turn back into soil for their garden.

The cemetery inside the I-85 cloverleaf at exit 35 is the John Coggin Meadows Cemetery. Meadows apparently bought the land in 1838 for $500.00. The property in Coweta County was passed down through the family and eventually sold many times, but always with the exception of a small plot at one corner of the lot—a section that came to be known as "the Old Meadows Cemetery."

When the Department of Transportation was planning the right of way for Interstate 85, surviving members of the Meadows Family objected to relocating the Cemetery. The DOT agreed to preserve it and, judging by the fresh flowers and new grave sites, it is still sacred ground to the family. But the garden-like atmosphere left when the Interstate highway arrived.

Honoring and remembering the departed is an important part of our culture. But cemeteries take up space. And someday when all who know us are gone, what will be the purpose? I wonder about our tenacious insistence on having an "eternal" resting place, as though that plot of ground is where we will reside for eternity.

A hundred years from now, nobody is going to be looking for my grave, anyway. The only problem might be that someone in Louisville, Kentucky—where I lived for a while—might visit Cave Hill Cemetery and mistake me for another James D. Porter. He died ninety years before I was born, and he was known as "the Kentucky Giant." He stood 7 feet 8 inches tall and weighed 300 pounds. I'm a foot shorter and a hundred pounds lighter than he was, and after a lifetime of being teased about my height, I don't particularly want to spend eternity being known as a "giant."

47

Letters from the Heart

Published June 14, 2022

Now that I live in Atlanta and many of my friends are in Albany, I should probably purchase some manly stationery and start writing letters. I could tell people about my new life in the big city and how challenging it is to start over late in life. I might write about the Saturday morning "Secret Garden" tour we signed up for or the Sunday evening Concert on the Green we attended—both within walking distance of our house.

I might also share a few of the challenges of living in a new city. Like getting lost on my first morning walk or not knowing where most of my possessions are. It took us a week to find the TV remote. Oddly, there is something Christmas-like in opening a cardboard box and being excited to find something useful or being disappointed in its contents.

We need to find new doctors, a new dentist, and new radio stations for the car. We're looking for the fastest routes to the bank, the hardware store, and—most importantly—the hospital. When we went to have the address changed on our driver licenses, we found ourselves in what I will kindly call an "unfamiliar" part of town. Google maps had directed us to the location outside a largely abandoned shopping mall and if there was a government office inside, they had neglected to place any signs on the building. We waited in the car for a few minutes before we got up the nerve to venture inside where we found the Department of Driver services and its friendly efficient employees. Appearances can be deceiving. There is so much to tell you about my new life I'm not sure where to begin.

Doug Gray from Fayetteville, Tennessee wrote about a project he calls "The Late, Great Letter Revival" in his May 23rd *Albany Herald* guest column. Receiving a timely letter from a coveted sender, Gray suggests, can induce a euphoria that compels us to rip open the envelope as we walk in from the mailbox. I want to write letters like that.

But writing letters is something of a lost art. A generation ago, soldiers wrote letters from the war, lovers penned heartfelt missives, and spies used letters to send coded messages. Letters have even become historic documents. GPB and History Channel programs always feature letters that provide insight into some famous person's opinions, activities, and frame of mind.

One of the most moving letters I have ever heard was written to his wife by Major Sullivan Ballou on July 14, 1861. It is on the website of the National Park Service, but I first heard it on Ken Burns' 1990 mini-series, The Civil War, when the letter was read by Paul Roebling with Jay Ungar's Ashokan Farewell playing in the background. Ironically, the letter was found in Major Ballou's belongings and not delivered until after his death.

"My very dear Sarah," the letter began. "The indications are very strong that we shall move in a few days — perhaps tomorrow. Lest I should not be able to write again, I feel impelled to write a few lines that may fall under your eye when I shall be no more."

Major Ballou's letter reads like poetry and is even prophetic when he asserts, "But, O Sarah! If the dead can come back to this earth and flit unseen around those they loved, I shall always be near you; in the gladdest days and in the darkest nights ... always, always, and if there be a soft breeze upon your cheek, it shall be my breath, as the cool air fans your throbbing temple, it shall be my spirit passing by. Sarah do not mourn me dead; think I am gone and wait for thee, for we shall meet again."

Sullivan Ballou was killed a week later on July 21, 1861, at the First Battle of Bull Run. His wife Sarah lived a long life and never remarried—perhaps because of Major Ballou's unseen spirit flitting around.

I wish I could write as well as Sullivan Ballou. But although my aging, arthritic hands can still hammer a nail, open a jar, and hug my wife, they are unsteady and shaky enough to render my handwriting almost illegible. I don't attempt handwritten letters because my cursive writing is more like Egyptian hieroglyphics.

I wonder what history will make of a 21st Century generation that doesn't write letters anymore. These days, we prefer to generate posts, texts, and emails that are brief, impulsive, and superficial. They are at once as ethereal as a summer breeze and as permanent as a wart. A letter is a heart-felt expression of emotion. A letter can last for generations, or you can burn it and make it go away. When you hit send on that electronic message, it is out there forever—whether you like it or not.

A happy birthday wish on social media is not the same as going to the store, picking out just the right card, and mailing it to a loved one with a note and a gift. And if you are thinking about wishing your spouse a happy anniversary on Facebook alone, you had better be ready to sleep on the couch.

I can still manage handwritten thank you notes. They are brief and essential to good manners. But handwriting a full length, multi-page letter seems insurmountable. So, why not just type my letters? Well, the truth is that I cannot type. That's right. Even though I have written countless stories for this newspaper, penned a couple of short non-fiction books and published two, seventy-thousand-word novels, I am, at best, a hunt-and-peck typist.

So here I am submitting one of my final columns from Atlanta to my friends in Albany and the surrounding areas. It contains my personal observations. It is from the heart. And it is meant to help me maintain connections. But thank goodness, it is not a handwritten letter. If it was, you might suspect that I am a spy writing in some secret code.

48

Cemeteries: Stories Etched in Stone

Published April 29, 2022

One of the things I miss about living in Albany, Georgia is my small-town notoriety. People stopped me on the street and in the stores all the time to comment on my articles. One such encounter occurred when a gentleman approached me in the shoe store. He had been waiting in his car for his wife when he spotted me walking in. He found me trying on a new pair of walking shoes.

The man had, it turned out, seen my articles on southern plantations and was reminded of a story that played out in Albany over a hundred years ago. He had read about it in the *Albany Herald* but had loaned the article to someone and never got it back. His memory was a little vague, but he wondered if I was familiar with the story. I was not, but I said I would look into it. I did, and here is what I discovered.

According to the *Memoirs of Judge Richard H. Clark*, published in 1898, Judge Clark was summoned to Albany, Georgia in March 1859 to join the prosecution of the killer of Mr. Joseph Bond. Bond's story sounds like the tale recalled by the man in the shoe store.

Joseph Bond was one of the wealthiest men in middle Georgia before the Civil War. He was the state's largest cotton grower and most successful planter. It was reported that in 1857, he set a world record with a cotton sale of 2,200 bales for $100,000. Bond was from Macon, but had holdings all over middle Georgia including, it would appear, in the Albany area at a place he called White Hill Plantation.

According to his contemporaries, Bond was not only a talented farmer and businessman, but he was also a man of the highest character and talent. "He was brave and courageous beyond measure. He could not brook an insult or submit tamely to a wrong."

When one of Bond's employees, an overseer by the name of Marshall Brown, beat one of Bond's slaves nearly to death, Bond fired the man and threatened to whip him if he ever touched one of his slaves again. Brown promptly found a job at a neighboring plantation, which put him in continuing contact with his former boss's slaves.

Brown, as the story goes, held a grudge against his former employer and found an opportunity to antagonize the man by once again beating one of his slaves. When Bond found out, he immediately rode out to confront Brown and, true to his word, commenced to beat the cruel overseer with a stick. Unfortunately for Joseph Bond, the overseer had the foresight to arm himself. Brown also made sure to have white witnesses present to testify that he was being beaten and acting in self-defense when he pulled out a small pistol and shot and killed his former boss. Joseph Bond was forty-four years old. Brown was tried in an Albany courtroom but never convicted of the killing.

Joseph Bond's contemporaries portrayed him as "a kind master." His slaves were "well clad, well fed, and well cared for." After his death, his former slaves supposedly spoke of him "with trembling accents of love and gratitude." I don't want to be an apologist for slave owners, but Bond was a man of his times, and he did die defending the honor of one of his slaves.

The person who killed Joseph Bond was a cruel, vindictive man who had severely beaten a slave and deliberately shot and killed the man who came to his defense. But he was acting in self-defense. It was a sad story for all involved—especially for any slaves who came under the lash of Marshall Brown.

The incident is recorded in Judge Clark's memoir (available at the Dougherty County Public Library). It is also recalled in detail at the Rose Hill Cemetery blog because, as I discovered, Joseph Bond is buried there.

Macon's Rose Hill Cemetery is a fifty-acre property located on the banks of the Ocmulgee River. It opened in 1840 and boasts the claim to fame as being the hangout and artistic inspiration for the Allman Brothers Band during their early years. In fact, Duane and Gregg Allman are buried there. The cemetery was developed outside of the city because the land was less expensive. It was originally designed to be both a cemetery and a local park.

People who visit Rose Hill Cemetery today might come across the Joseph Bond grave site and be impressed with the memorial's size and beauty. They might also do a bit of quick math and discover that he was only in his forties when he died. But they will need to inquire further to learn the rest of the story—something I might never have known but for a chance encounter in a shoe store.

Cemeteries are more than just places to lay our loved ones to rest. They are as important to our communities as parks, libraries, and town centers. They are historical archives. When I visited Albany's Oakview Cemetery, I was impressed with the burial plot of Nelson Tift and his family, but I already knew his story. He was the founder of Albany and the employer of the former slave and bridge builder, Horace King.

I was struck, however, as I explored the tragic story of Joseph Bond that Nelson Tift was in Albany when the incident played out. I wonder if their paths ever crossed. Joseph Bond was murdered near Albany in March 1859, the year after Horace King completed the bridge house and its crossing of the Flint River. But if there is a story there, I can find no record of it. Cemeteries only give us the headlines.

Another intriguing but untold story surrounds a simple, unassuming grave in the cemetery my wife and I recently explored in Decatur, Georgia. The Decatur Cemetery, we discovered, is the oldest burial ground in the Atlanta metropolitan area. The earliest headstones date to the 1820s, predating the city of Atlanta itself by more than a decade. The cemetery is Decatur's largest downtown greenspace—a quiet park that covers about fifty-eight acres and contains well over 20,000 graves. The landscaping and monuments in the eight-acre Old Section are historically significant and include the graves of local dignitaries, numerous Civil War veterans, and a man named John Hays.

Hays was born on November 2, 1751, and he died June 17, 1829. In 1776, Hays would have been twenty-five years old. He was, according to his marker, a veteran of the Revolutionary War. How did this contemporary of George Washington come to be buried in Decatur Georgia and what was his role in the Revolutionary War? Maybe that's a story for another time.

We can wander among the monuments, headstones, and markers, looking for stories. We can remember heroes and ordinary people, enslaved people and their enslavers, people who lived long lives and children who died too young. The stories may be personal or just a collective memory of our community. But cemeteries are a touching reminder of our own mortality because, at the end of the day, whether etched on a stone monument in a cemetery or simply carved into the hearts of loved ones left behind, we will all have an epitaph.

I'm not sure how I would like to be remembered. I like the humorous gravestones, like the one that recalls the famous "I see dead people" line from the 1999 movie *The Sixth Sense*. One tombstone changes the language of that quote and perhaps gives us a glimpse into the afterlife when it says, "I see dumb people." Another tombstone says, "Here lies an atheist. All dressed up and no place to go."

Since I wish to be cremated or composted, I don't plan to have a tombstone. If I did, I would probably just keep it simple—perhaps something like Mel Blanc's epitaph. The voice of Bugs Bunny and a thousand other cartoon characters has on his tombstone: "That's All Folks."